HURRY UP
and WAIT

HURRY UP
and WAIT

Hawai'i's Favorite Recipes
for the Pressure Cooker and the Slow Cooker

by Betty Shimabukuro and Joleen Oshiro

Mutual
Publishing

Library of Congress Control Number: 2018934986

ISBN: 978-1939487-08-7

First Printing, October 2013
Second Printing, January 2015
Third Printing, July 2018

Mutual Publishing, LLC
1215 Center Street, Suite 210
Honolulu, Hawai'i 96816
Ph: 808-732-1709 | Fax: 808-734-4094
email: info@mutualpublishing.com
www.mutualpublishing.com

Printed in South Korea

Photography by Jamm Aquino: pg. 135
Photography by Christina Chun: pgs. 9, 19, 27, 39, 41, 47, 49, 51, 53, 61, 63, 74, 75
Photography by Bryant Fukutomi: pgs. 25, 34, 36, 73
Photography by George Lee: pgs. xiii, xvii
Photography by Krystle Marcellus : pg. 153
Photography by F. L. Morris: pg. 96
Photography by Joleen Oshiro: pg. xiii
Photography by Cindy Ellen Russell: pg. 136
Photography by Betty Shimabukuro: pgs. xviii, 4, 7, 9, 11, 31, 87, 89, 91, 93, 99, 103, 109, 110, 107, 115, 119, 121, 125, 127, 129, 139, 141, 131, 133, 134, 145, 147, 149, 151, 154
Photos from Dreamstime.com: pg. 2 © Klenova, pg. 6 © Elena Elisseeva, pg. 18 © Taviphoto, pg. 21 © ianghongyan, pg. 26 © Photooasis, pg. 33 © Jumnong, pg. 37 © Sally Scott, pg. 45 © Zkruger, pg. 48 © Inga Nielsen, pg. 52 © Norman Chan, pg. 56 © Jill Chen, pg. 58 © Antonio Ribeiro, pg. 71 © Robyn Mackenzie, pg. 72 © Richard Griffin, pg. 80 (top) © Viktorfischer, pg. 80 (bottom) © Radub85, pg. 106 © Travelling-light, pg. 117 © Msphotographic
Photos from iStockphotography.com: pg. 84 © Kheng Guan Toh, pg. 124 © IslandLeigh
Cover Design by Jane Gillespie
Design by Courtney Tomasu

Star ★ Advertiser
HONOLULU

"News you can use" is an old newspaper adage that emphasizes the role a good publication plays in helping readers negotiate the tasks of life. Our front page may be filled with the breaking news of the day, but on other pages we tell you where to get great saimin. Or how to bake a cake in your Crock-Pot, or how to cut meal-time prep in half with a pressure cooker.

Hurry Up and Wait—by *Honolulu Star-Advertiser* food writers Betty Shimabukuro and Joleen Oshiro—dishes up a hearty serving of news you can use to anyone who cooks or loves to eat. Life is hectic. The slow cooker and the pressure cooker can make it less so.

We invite you to step into the kitchen with us, whether you'd like to cook it fast or cook it slow.

ALOHA,
Dennis Francis
President and publisher,
Honolulu Star-Advertiser
and Oʻahu Publications

Contents

SLOW RECIPES

The Soup Pot

Veggies & Sides

Enter the Entrée

BEEF

CHICKEN

Acknowledgments

FAST COOKING // JOLEEN OSHIRO

Compiling the material for this collection of recipes would not have been possible without the support of some key people. Foremost, I'd like to thank chef Alyssa Moreau for teaching me skills that enabled me to find success with the pressure cooker. Her willingness to share her knowledge made the task of crafting recipes less daunting and more enjoyable. My heartfelt gratitude goes out to chef Grant Sato for his support of all my food-related work and for allowing me to publish a couple of his delicious recipes. Alyssa, Kathleen Freitas, Pomai Souza, Joe and Sally Aguinaldo, and Walter Rhee also were kind enough to contribute recipes, and I appreciate their generosity.

Thanks to Christina Chun and Bryant Fukutomi for their photography.

And thanks to my husband, Noel, and daughter, Mia, for washing countless dishes as I tested recipes over and over again. And finally, deep appreciation goes to Betty Shimabukuro for mentoring and partnering with me on this project, and to my mother, Ethel Oshiro, whose wonderful dishes continue to provide me a reference point for good food.

SLOW COOKING // BETTY SHIMABUKURO

Several readers of the *Honolulu Star-Advertiser* contributed ideas in my search for slow-cooker recipes. Many thanks to Steve Dung, Hayley Matson-Mathes, Melissa Pang Nikaido, Joanne Naai, Keith Okazaki, Rose Soto, and Jane Wakukawa, as well as chefs Wade Ueoka and Beth An Nishijima. All contributed recipes used or adapted for this book.

Introduction

This book has a split personality. That much is obvious from the theme: It's about cooking fast and cooking slow in two different appliances by two different writers. We're not going to pretend we wrote this book as one or that we're equally versed in both cooking forms. We're not.

This is what we are: Two writers from the Food section of the *Honolulu Star-Advertiser* who began experimenting with these kitchen tools largely as part of our reporting duties, and in doing so discovered how the pressure cooker (for Joleen) and the slow cooker (for Betty) could make life easier and tastier.

We're both living typical not-enough-hours-in-the-day lives, spending too much time commuting on the H-1, juggling jobs and families, trying to feed those families without an over-reliance on takeout or packaged foods. Neither cooker can magically solve this dilemma, but both can produce island-style favorites in efficient and consistent ways, which goes a long way toward easing everyday stress.

This book is written in two distinct voices, by design, as these obviously are very different cooking tools. We've found that many people who have pressure cookers or slow cookers rarely use them because of unimpressive past results or because they just can't get the hang of incorporating either device into daily life. And so, for many months—and often with the help of our readers—we've been working on local-style recipes that make the best use of these two devices. We've made the mistakes that can sabotage a home cook, so you don't have to.

This book comprises the best of our discoveries.

Cook it fast, cook it slow, do a little of both. You'll be able to pressure-cook a meal of Ma Po Tofu in about three minutes; or put a Liliko'i Cheesecake on the potluck table and announce that you made it in your Crock-Pot.

Amaze yourself. Amaze your family and friends.

BETTY SHIMABUKURO & JOLEEN OSHIRO

Wiki Cooking

JOLEEN OSHIRO

t was a couple of years ago that I was introduced to the wonders of the pressure cooker while writing a food story for the *Honolulu Star-Advertiser*. Here was a device, I was told, that could deliver stew in 20 minutes or a roast in an hour. Be still my beating heart! Like so many working folks, commuting to and from town for work, and in my case, driving a child to school across the island, my family ate way too many fast-food meals. It was a strain on our pocketbook, not to mention our health, and I felt awful that our dinners were at odds with locavore values.

So, not long after that story published, I purchased my first pressure cooker, a six-quart Fagor brand pot for which I got a double discount and a rebate—a $100 cooker for $30. As do most brands, Fagor says its cookers decrease cooking time by at least 30 percent, and I've found this to be true.

Here are some things to know about pressure cookers.

How a pressure cooker works:

- The pressure cooker offers a faster cooking process, between 30 and 70 percent less cooking time. When its lid is sealed and locked, steam produced by heating liquid builds pressure, and that pressure raises the boiling temperature from 212 to 250°F. The increase in temperature breaks down food fibers about one-third faster than standard cooking. And because of the sealed environment, more nutrients and flavors stay within the food rather than escaping with the steam.

- This manner of cooking saves energy as well. Here's why: After a pot hits high pressure, heat must be lowered to regulate pressure, lest the dish burn and the cooker suffer damage. Lower heat plus shorter cooking time equals less energy use.

Types of pressure cookers:

- My pot has a spring-valve pressure regulator, which involves a colored cylinder that pops up to indicate when pressure is reached. Another type is the "jiggle-top" in which a metal weight sits on the cooker's vent pipe. When the pot hits pressure, the weight jiggles. A third resembles a jiggle-top, but the regulator doesn't jiggle, requiring that the pot be carefully monitored to determine when it reaches pressure.

- All types have safety latches that cannot be unlocked until pressure is released. This prevents the explosions of food that occurred with pressure cookers of the past.

Important features:

- Find a cooker that operates at fourteen to sixteen pounds per square inch (psi) when it hits high pressure, since the standard pressure used in recipes is fifteen psi. Lower psi can substantially extend cooking time. Good-quality pots are constructed of 18/10 stainless steel and have three-ply bottoms that include a layer of aluminum or copper to promote even heating, which is important to prevent scorching.

Cooking tips:

- Because steam is vital to the cooking process, most pressure cookers require one-half to one cup of liquid in the pot when in use. While selecting a pot, look for one that won't require much more liquid, or dishes could end up watery.

- Fill pots no more than two-thirds full. There needs to be space in the cavity for pressure to build.

- The pressure cooker is an ideal way to cook beans. Not only does it dramatically decrease cooking time, it delivers beans that are well cooked without loss of flavor. When preparing beans, fill the pot no more than halfway, and add a tablespoon or two of oil to control the foam that is produced during the cooking process. Many online pressure-cooking sites and cookbooks recommend presoaking beans, but I never do. I just follow my resource for cooking times: a chart composed by author Lorna Sass, in my personal pressure-cooking bible, *Pressure Perfect*. (She includes charts for meats, vegetables and grains as well in her cookbooks.) Most pressure cookers come with manuals or cookbooks that include general cooking times.

- There are several ways to release pressure, depending on how much residual cooking time a dish requires, because food continues to cook in a pressurized environment with high temperature even when the pot is removed from the heat source.

- One way to finish off the cooking process is to allow the pot to come to a "natural-pressure release," meaning the lid remains sealed until the pot cools enough for pressure to diffuse. This method is used regularly for cooking proteins and beans.

- Quick-pressure release involves opening a valve on the cooker. But the fastest way to release pressure is to run water from a faucet over the lid of the pot. Within seconds, pressure is diffused. This method allows for proper cooking of vegetables that would otherwise end up overcooked.

Accessories and tools:

- Use inserts to expand the possibilities of pressure cooking. Trivets, which raise a pan or bowl off the bottom of the pot, allow for cooking casserole-type dishes or foods that would overcook or burn if heated directly in the pot. Some foods are best cooked in foil packets on a trivet or in a steamer basket. These include fish fillets, or potatoes to be added to longer-cooking stews or curries.

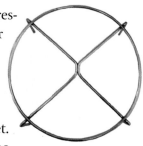

- When cooking something in a bowl or pan, use foil strips to retrieve the dish from the heated pot. This tip comes from Sass: Cut two long pieces aluminum foil. Fold them crosswise to make long strips. Lay the strips over the trivet across each other to form an "x," so four strips are coming out of the pot. Place the dish on top of the strips. Tuck the ends into the pot, cover and seal. When food is done, straighten out the four foil strips and grab them to lift out the dish.

Important food notes (also courtesy of Sass):

When adding tomato products to the pot, pour them over the rest of the ingredients rather than mixing them in, as they tend to burn easily. And garlic powder is a wonderful substitute for fresh garlic, which tends to disintegrate under pressure without leaving its flavor behind.

Slo 'Ono

BETTY SHIMABUKURO

For decades I tried to develop a meaningful relationship with my slow cooker, but it was an inconsistent partner. A great meal here, a mediocre one there. Rapture and rejection for so many years.

Sometime in 2010 I decided, enough of that. I looked my Crock-Pot square in the eye (which is somewhere around the temperature knob) and said, "Prove yourself to me, or I am turning your space over to a food processor."

The pot having no free will or opposable thumbs, however, meant the proving was left to me. I spent months combing cookbooks and searching online sources, and I tried to use the dang thing once a week.

In 2011 I launched a Crock-Pot crusade in the *Honolulu Star-Advertiser* that became known as "Slow 'Ono." My goal: great, uncomplicated local-style slow-cooker meals. Readers were invited to submit recipes and requests, and I reported my top finds once a month. Those recipes became the start of this cookbook.

Why bother? Because a slow cooker can save money and energy. It allows you to cook a meal while absent from the house, which saves time even as it takes time. Nothing boils over and nothing burns (unless you are very neglectful). And low-heat, long cooking is supposed to be the best way to draw the most out of many foods.

Why is it so difficult? We expect too much from this partner. We want to toss some ingredients in the crock, turn it on, go to work, come home, and scoop out dinner, preferably delicious. We seek the holy grail—a dish that is at its prime after ten hours of cooking, equal to an eight-hour workday, plus commute. We want it to be effortless.

It is this singular pursuit that leaves so many people dissatisfied with their slow cookers. Truth is, most dishes peak after six to eight hours of cooking (less for chicken), with overcooking leading to blah results. And sometimes a dish is improved by attention midway through, such as turning the meat or adding ingredients, especially vegetables, that have shorter cooking times.

As for effortless? Often you'll be much happier with the finished product if you do a little bit of tweaking afterward (skim the fat, thicken the sauce, sometimes even broil the meat to give it some crusty chew).

Treat your slow cooker as a tool, not a solo workhorse, one that sometimes needs the assist of the range or microwave, and some understanding from you.

The two of you will be much happier together.

Choosing a slow cooker:

The two most common brands are Crock-Pot and Hamilton Beach. Both companies offer many models—from $20 to $200, with all kinds of features. All basically cook at two temperature settings, low and high, with a warm setting for finished dishes. They are simple machines, although some have timers, temperature sensors, even browning elements.

The recipes in this book were tested in basic models of both brands. If you are buying your first, I would suggest a six- or seven-quart oval cooker, which is of a size and shape that can accommodate a large roast. If you need something smaller for a particular recipe you can place a casserole dish inside the crock. You can get along without any other bells or whistles.

If you find you have an affinity for slow cooking you can investigate a fancier model.

Other helpful tools:

- A good gravy separator, one that can hold at least four cups and has a cover that strains out solids. Removing fat from the juices in your crock leads to better sauces and gravies.

- A 1.5- or 2-quart round ceramic baking dish or casserole. This should fit inside your slow cooker. It is handy for recipes designed for smaller cookers and for many desserts.

- A spaghetti spoon, sometimes called a pasta fork, strainer, or server. A cross between a slotted spoon and a claw, this tool is efficient at scooping out the contents of your crock while leaving the liquid behind.

- A miniature slow cooker. These 1.5- to 2-quart babies provide the advantages of slow cooking without the bulk. Basic models can be found for as little as $10 and are perfect for many desserts or reduced versions of standard recipes—a small amount of stew, for example. They are also great for making soup stock. Take the bones from your pork chop dinner, add water and cook all night. Tomorrow you'll have two or three cups of a nice stock.

{ Kickoff Cookoff }

A number of dishes considered standard fare in any local recipe lineup are well-suited for both the slow cooker and the pressure cooker. Four—Chicken Adobo, Chicken Long Rice, Shoyu Chicken, and Portuguese Bean Soup—are profiled here with recipes tailored for both appliances. While each recipe is distinctive, all exemplify the flavors that make these dishes all-time favorites.

If you have a slow cooker but no pressure cooker, or vice versa, compare these recipes. You may be persuaded to invite the other appliance into your home.

Chicken Adobo

SERVES 6 TO 8

While researching this Filipino dish, I couldn't believe its simplicity, reiterated in recipe after recipe. It's basically a combination of a few common ingredients in which the chicken is marinated, then cooked. While marinating takes several hours, cooking in the pressure cooker is only about 10 minutes. If you like, when the cooking is complete, turn up the heat and reduce the sauce. Adobo has a strong, bright flavor out of the pot, then settles into a lovely mellowness the next day.

4 to 5 pounds chicken thighs
½ cup white vinegar
½ cup soy sauce
1 tablespoon garlic powder
1 teaspoon peppercorns
3 bay leaves
1 tablespoon brown sugar

In bowl, combine ingredients well, then cover and marinate in refrigerator at least 1 hour, preferably 3 hours.

Transfer ingredients to pot. Cover, seal lid, and bring to pressure. Reduce heat and cook 8 to 10 minutes.

Remove from heat, allow natural-pressure release for 4 minutes, then quick-release pressure. Chicken should fall off the bone easily.

Chicken Adobo

SERVES 6

The usual local version of adobo is chicken or pork simmered in a simple vinegar-based sauce. Traditional Filipino recipes will sometimes include coconut milk or sugar—and they often call for broiling, grilling or frying the meat at the end to crisp the outside.

This recipe calls for marinating as a first step, and in the end broiling the chicken and thickening the sauce. All this is meant to intensify the flavor, but if it's too fussy for you, just throw all the ingredients in the crock and cook. Eat it straight out of the pot. You'll still be satisfied.

4 pounds chicken thighs, skin removed, bone-in (see note)
1 large onion, sliced
1 teaspoon pepper
3 tablespoons tapioca starch or cornstarch dissolved in
    3 tablespoons water

Marinade:

1½ cups cider vinegar
½ cup soy sauce
3 cloves garlic, minced

Combine marinade ingredients. Pour over chicken pieces and let marinate, refrigerated, at least 4 hours.

Place onions in bottom of slow cooker. Top with chicken and sprinkle with pepper. Pour marinade over all. Cook on low 4 to 5 hours, until chicken is tender. Turn pieces halfway through, if possible.

(If cooking ahead to serve on another day, refrigerate chicken and onions separately from juices. When ready to serve, remove fat from sauce and proceed with the next steps.)

continued on the next page

Place chicken on broiling pan and broil 5 minutes per side until lightly browned.

Meanwhile, skim fat from liquid in slow cooker. Place liquid in small pot on stove; bring to simmer. Dissolve tapioca or cornstarch in water and stir into pot, continuing to stir until mixture thickens. Serve chicken with onions and pour sauce over all.

{ FOR PORK ADOBO } The same marinade can be used with pieces of pork cut in cubes. Cooking time will be 4 to 6 hours.

{ NOTE } Removing the skin from chicken pieces helps cut the fat in the dish, but if left on the skin crisps up under the broiler. Your choice.

Chicken Long Rice

SERVES 6

A t my house, we don't need a spread of laulau, kālua pig, and lomi salmon to enjoy Chicken Long Rice. We eat it by itself and treat it like soup. In fact, it's one of my daughter's favorite comfort foods. Add plenty of ginger, and it's a great dish for someone under the weather. Though this recipe offers an option for incorporating chicken broth, it doesn't take much ambition or effort to make the broth from scratch, just 30 minutes of pressure cooking chicken wings, back, neck, or bones. For a broth with a touch of sweetness, add some carrots. While all this is happening, soak the long rice in boiling water, then simply add it in at the end and simmer 5 minutes. That way, you'll preserve the soupy quality of the dish.

2 (2-ounce) bundles long rice
3 quarts water (or substitute 3 to 4 cans chicken broth, or a
    combo of water and canned broth)
2½ pounds bone-in chicken pieces
1 large onion, diced
3 tablespoons salt, or to taste (reduce salt if using canned broth)
3 to 4 shiitake mushrooms, soaked in water until soft, and sliced,
    stems removed; reserve water
2 tablespoons soy sauce
1 finger-size piece ginger, peeled and smashed, or to taste
1 tablespoon garlic powder, or to taste
Bamboo shoots (optional)
3 stalks green onion, chopped, for garnish

In large bowl, soak long rice bundles in boiling water. Set aside.

To pressure cooker pot, add water, chicken, onion, salt, shiitake and its reserved water, and soy sauce. Seal lid, bring to pressure, lower heat, and cook 10 minutes.

continued on the next page

Quick-release pressure and remove chicken. Shred or remove meat from bone and slice into bite-sized pieces. Set aside.

Return bones to pot, add ginger and garlic powder; seal lid. Bring to pressure, lower heat, and cook 30 minutes.

Quick-release pressure, strain out bones, and return broth and pot to burner. Taste broth and adjust seasoning. Return chicken to pot.

Drain long rice and add to pot along with bamboo shoots if using. Cover with lid but do not seal. Simmer 5 minutes. Serve with topping of green onion.

Chicken Long Rice

SERVES 8

*T*his is a dish I usually skip at the lūʻau table. I've always found it a bit blah compared with the bold flavors offered by other dishes. But this version, built on a broth made with a few chicken thighs and just a bit of ginger, is much tastier than the average. It is clear evidence of how a little extra effort yields much better slow-cooker results.

6 chicken thighs, bone-in, skin and excess fat removed
2-inch piece ginger, peeled, sliced, smashed
2 cups water
4 ounces long rice or bean thread noodles (2 small packages),
    soaked in water to soften
4 cups watercress (leaves and thin stems only; discard thick
    stems)

Place chicken and ginger in 5- or 6-quart slow cooker, add water. Cook on low 4 hours or until chicken is very tender (do not overcook or texture will suffer). Remove chicken, debone, and shred.

Add long rice and watercress to crock. Turn off and let sit 15 minutes. Noodles will absorb most of the liquid and watercress will wilt. Stir in shredded chicken.

Portuguese Bean Soup

SERVES 8

The inspiration for this recipe came from a friendly stranger I chatted with in the supermarket. While I was perusing kabocha, she shared that one of the best things she makes with the pumpkin is Portuguese bean soup. Though at first thought that might seem odd, kabocha contributes a mellow sweetness that adds a subtle depth of flavor. Just a small amount, diced very small so that it melts into the broth, makes a world of difference, she insisted. Then she pointed at the kale and said there wasn't any better green to add to the pot. I've tested this recipe on various friends and relatives, and they agree.

2 cups dried navy beans
15 cups water, divided
2 tablespoons oil, divided
1 large onion, diced
1 cup celery, diced
2 medium carrots, diced
1 (10-ounce) Portuguese sausage, peeled of casing and cubed
3 to 4 hamhocks
½ cup kabocha, small dice
1 (14.5-ounce) can diced tomatoes
1 (8-ounce) can tomato sauce
2 medium potatoes, large dice
Salt and pepper, to taste
1 bunch kale, sliced into strips

Cook beans: Place beans into pressure-cooker pot. Add 6 cups water and 1 tablespoon oil. Seal lid, bring to pressure, lower heat, and cook 20 minutes. Remove from heat and allow natural-pressure release, about 20 minutes. Drain beans in colander and set aside.

On medium-high, heat rest of oil in pressure-cooker pot and add onions, celery and carrots. Sauté until onions soften. Remove to bowl and set aside.

Return pot to stove on medium-high heat and cook sausage. Remove to plate lined with paper towel and set aside.

Return pot to stove on high and add hamhocks, kabocha, and remaining 9 cups water. Seal lid, bring to pressure, lower heat, and cook 45 minutes. Remove from heat and allow natural-pressure release. Meat should be tender enough to fall off the bone. If not, reseal lid, return to heat, and cook another 10 minutes. Continue to check on hocks and cook until meat is extremely tender. Remove hocks from pot, shred or slice meat, discard bones, and return meat to pot.

Add diced tomatoes, tomato sauce, potatoes, and salt and pepper. Seal lid, bring to pressure, lower heat, and cook 1 minute. Quick-release pressure. Add kale, onion, carrots, and celery, reseal lid, bring to pressure, and quick-release pressure.

Open lid, and return navy beans and sausage to the pot. Simmer several minutes to reheat. Taste and adjust seasoning if necessary.

Portuguese Bean Soup

SERVES 10

A couple of inexpensive ham hocks are the great beginnings of the best bean soup you will ever make. You start in the morning making a fabulous pork broth, then continue using that broth as the basis of your soup.

If you have a ham at Thanksgiving, this is a great Black Friday soup. Start the stock, using the ham bone, before going to bed. In the morning make the soup and let it cook all day while everyone's out and about. They all can feed themselves when they get home.

2 (15-ounce) cans kidney beans, with liquid, or ½ pound dry beans
2 cups diced tomatoes (fresh or canned)
1 large onion, halved and cut in wedges
1 large potato, peeled and diced in ½-inch pieces (about 2 cups)
2 large carrots, peeled and sliced ½-inch thick (about 2 cups)
1 (15-ounce) can tomato sauce
12 ounces Portuguese sausage, in 1-inch slices
6 cups shredded kale

Stock:

2 ham hocks (or a leftover ham bone)
1 sprig rosemary
1 cup coarsely chopped cilantro (leaves and stems)
3 cloves garlic, peeled and crushed
3 cups water, or more as needed

Combine stock ingredients in 6-quart slow-cooker. Add more water if needed to cover hocks. Cook on low at least 4 hours (longer cooking is OK, so you can let it simmer overnight).

If using dry beans, soak in water overnight; drain.

Remove ham hocks; debone, and chop meat, discarding large pieces of fat. Refrigerate meat.

Remove liquid from pot, strain and skim fat. Return 2 cups stock to pot if using canned beans; 3 cups if using dry. Reserve any remaining stock for another use (makes a great base for stew or another soup).

Add beans to pot along with all of the vegetables and tomato sauce. Continue cooking on low 8 hours, or until vegetables and beans are tender. Soup will hold on warm for several hours. Stir in cooked meat, sausage, and kale and cook another 30 minutes or until meat is heated through and kale is tender.

{ TO SIMPLIFY } If you don't have all day for this, or if you can't be home after 4 hours to tend the pot, just put everything in at once (except the kale) and let it go for 8 to 10 hours. The stock won't be as flavorful, but what you don't know you can't miss.

Shoyu Chicken

SERVES 8

*F*ew dishes are more popular with the local crowd than Shoyu Chicken, an ultimate Hawai'i-style comfort food. Thanks to the pressure cooker, this staple can be on the weekday dinner table, flavorful and fork tender, in 30 minutes from beginning to end.

1 tablespoon olive oil
5 pounds chicken thighs, skin and fat removed
1 large onion, large dice
1¼ cups soy sauce
¼ cup water
1 cup brown sugar
1½ tablespoons garlic powder
½ to 1 teaspoon rock salt
1 finger ginger, peeled and smashed
2 tablespoons cornstarch, mixed with 2 tablespoons water

Place oil in pot and heat on high. Add chicken and onions and brown.

Meanwhile, in bowl, combine soy sauce, water, sugar, garlic powder, salt and ginger. Pour over chicken. Seal lid and on high heat bring pot to pressure. Lower heat and cook 15 minutes.

Remove pot from heat. Allow natural-pressure release for 4 minutes, then quick-release pressure. Open lid and test a piece of chicken with a fork; meat should easily flake with gentle pressure. If chicken isn't tender, pressure cook another 2 minutes.

Skim fat off top of sauce, or refrigerate chicken overnight and remove solidified fat.

When ready to eat, heat chicken and sauce. Remove chicken to serving bowl. Bring sauce to boil and add cornstarch mixture. Simmer, stirring until sauce is thickened, 2 to 3 minutes. Pour over chicken.

Shoyu Chicken
SERVES 6

he trick to really good Shoyu Chicken was taught to me by Paul Masuoka, owner of the now defunct Masu's Massive Plate Lunch. He said to brown the chicken really well on really high heat—we're talking near-charred here. If your smoke detector goes off, you know you're doing it right, he told me. I do this on a portable gas burner outside—I'm not sure I know how to turn off my smoke detector.

4 to 5 pounds chicken thighs, skin removed, bone-in
¼ cup water

Marinade:

½ cup soy sauce
¼ cup mirin (sweet Japanese cooking wine)
¼ cup brown sugar
3 cloves garlic, crushed and minced
1-inch piece ginger, crushed and minced
½ cup chopped cilantro, leaves and stems

Combine marinade ingredients. Pour over chicken. Marinate 4 hours in refrigerator.

Place large skillet over high heat. Remove chicken from marinade (reserving all the marinade). Brown chicken well. Remove chicken to to 6- or 7-quart slow cooker.

Add water to skillet and deglaze (scrape up the browned bits at bottom of pan). Pour contents of skillet over chicken along with all the reserved marinade. Cook on low 4 to 5 hours or until cooked through. Turn pieces halfway through.

To thicken sauce (optional): Remove chicken pieces and skim fat from liquid in crock. Thicken sauce on stove top using a slurry of 3 tablespoons cornstarch or tapioca starch dissolved in ¼ cup water.

FAST RECIPES
FOR THE PRESSURE COOKER

{ The Soup Pot }

Soups lend themselves to pressure cooking because the cooker cuts down the time traditionally spent on everything from cooking beans to making stock. It takes just 30 to 60 minutes of pressure cooking bones to create delicious homemade stock. (Smaller bones, such as those from chicken, take less time than thick beef bones.) Add some aromatic vegetables if you want to round out the flavor.

Chicken Jasmine Rice Jook

SERVES 6 TO 8

hanks to its delicate grain and appealing fragrance, jasmine rice makes for an exceptionally friendly jook recipe: It cooks up quickly and delivers lots of flavor. Jook is a favorite post-Thanksgiving comfort dish that utilizes turkey bones and leftover meat. But in this recipe I use chicken instead, a natural substitute. Tailor this basic recipe with your favorite add-ins. Some of the possibilities include shelled raw peanuts, fishcake, black mushrooms, and bamboo shoots. Of course, whether it's a turkey or chicken jook, plain or fancy, the dish isn't complete without a healthy topping of Chinese parsley.

5 cups water
2 (14.5-ounce) cans chicken broth
1 pound bone-in chicken thighs or legs, skin removed and trimmed
  of fat
1 cup jasmine rice
1 finger ginger, peeled and smashed
2 tablespoons soy sauce
1 tablespoon salt
Green onions, for garnish
Chinese parsley, for garnish

Combine all ingredients, except green onions and Chinese parsley, in pressure cooker and seal lid. On high heat, bring pot to pressure, then lower heat, and cook 20 minutes.

Quick-release pressure under running tap. Fish out chicken, shred meat, and return to pot. Discard bones. Taste and adjust seasoning if necessary.

Serve with green onions and parsley.

Lentil-Vegetable Soup

SERVES 8

I created this recipe more than a decade ago when my daughter was a baby. It was the perfect nourishment when she was sick—hearty yet easy to digest. Some of my favorite ingredients in this soup are the kabocha and kale. The former lends a subtle touch of sweetness and thickens the broth. (Folks who want more sweetness can add some honey.) The latter is a healthful dark, leafy green that adds great color and texture and holds up well to reheating. Beyond that, add or replace any vegetables you want.

½ cup split peas
8 cups water
½ cup red lentils (or any other type of lentil)
3 tablespoons olive oil, divided
1 large onion, large diced
1 cup kabocha, half small dice, half diced
1 bunch kale, sliced into strips, with stems
   chopped into small pieces and separated
   from leaves
1 tablespoon rock salt, or to taste
1 tablespoon garlic powder
½ finger ginger, smashed
2 bay leaves
1 (14.5-ounce) can vegetable or chicken broth
1 medium zucchini, quartered and sliced about 2-inches thick
2 stalks celery, chopped
1 (14.5-ounce) can diced tomatoes (optional)
1 to 2 tablespoons honey, or to taste (optional)

Place split peas in pot with water and 1 tablespoon of the oil. Seal pot and bring to pressure. Lower heat and cook 7 minutes, then quick-release pressure.

Add lentils, seal pot, and bring to pressure. Lower heat and cook 5 minutes. Take pot off heat and allow natural-pressure release.

Use hand mixer in pot to partially blend soup. Or remove two-thirds of peas and lentils to blender and blend, then return to pot.

Add onions, small-diced kabocha, kale stems, salt, garlic powder, ginger, bay leaves, and broth. Seal lid, bring to pressure, lower heat, and cook 1 minute. Quick-release pressure.

Add kale leaves, remaining kabocha, zucchini, celery, and diced tomatoes if using. Seal lid again, bring to pressure, lower heat, and cook another minute. Quick-release pressure under running tap.

Add honey if using, mix, and taste. Adjust seasoning if necessary. Add remaining 2 tablespoons olive oil. Mix into soup and serve.

Soon Doo Bu
(Korean Tofu Stew)

SERVES 4

After deciding I wanted a recipe for Korean tofu stew in this collection, I didn't have to think twice about whom to ask: local cooking instructor Walter Rhee, who's gained a following for his Asian cooking classes and Chinatown food tours. (Visit www.waltereatshawaii.com.) I'm excited to include this dish because it calls for authentic Korean ingredients such as gochu garu (Korean pepper flakes) and myul-chi (large dried Korean anchovies). These items aren't readily available in supermarkets; instead, go to Korean grocers such as Keeaumoku and Palama markets. The proper way of serving soon doo bu, says Rhee, is to ladle it over rice in the style of a loco moco.

2 tablespoons vegetable oil
2½ cups chopped kim chee, squeezed to remove liquid
2 to 3 fresh shucked oysters, quick-rinsed in fresh water (optional)
1 stalk finely chopped green onion
½ tablespoon minced garlic
¼ pound julienned pork
½ teaspoon sea salt
½ teaspoon sesame oil
½ teaspoon ground black pepper
1½ tablespoons gochu garu (Korean red pepper flakes)
3 cups stock
1 block soft tofu
1 tablespoon flour mixed with ½ cup cold water
1 egg

Stock:

½ cup myul-chi (Korean dried large size anchovies)
⅓ cup daikon chunks
¼ cup dried shiitake mushrooms
1 (2 x 2-inch) piece konbu
4 cups water

Make stock first: Combine all ingredients in pressure cooker. Seal lid, bring to pressure on high, reduce heat and cook 5 minutes. Quick-release pressure, strain stock, and discard solids. Set aside.

In pot on medium heat, add cooking oil and stir-fry kim chee, oysters if using, green onion, garlic, pork, salt, sesame oil, pepper, and gochu garu, until pork is cooked.

Add stock and bring to boil, then add tofu, whole or broken into pieces. Bring pot to boil again.

Add flour mixture to thicken soup; bring to boil. Crack raw egg into soup before serving.

{ Veggies & Sides }

Side dishes can make a main dish shine or they can stand on their own as a light meal. The following array of pressure cooker dishes illustrates the many ways the appliance lends efficiency to preparation.

In making taro cake, the cooker saves time every step of the way in a dish that usually takes an investment of many hours. Miso Eggplant, meanwhile, can be turned around in a fraction of an hour. Cauliflower Casserole demonstrates how pressure cooking can serve as one step in a larger preparation process.

Okinawan
Sweet Potato Salad

SERVES 4 TO 6

The pressure cooker dramatically decreases the time it takes to make this colorful, healthy version of potato salad. It combines the sweetness of the potato with vibrant touches of ginger, lime, curry, and Dijon mustard, plus the crunch of red bell peppers and celery.

3 pounds Okinawan sweet potatoes, scrubbed
⅛ to ¼ teaspoon grated ginger, or to taste
1 tablespoon fresh lime juice
½ cup plain Greek yogurt
¼ to ½ cup mayonnaise, or to taste
2 teaspoons Dijon mustard
1 tablespoon curry powder
1 cup diced celery (about 2 stalks)
½ cup diced red bell pepper
¼ cup sweet onion, finely diced (optional)
½ teaspoon salt, or to taste
½ teaspoon pepper, or to taste

Place potatoes in pressure cooker with 1 cup of water. Seal lid, bring to pressure on high heat, then lower heat and cook 8 minutes.

Meanwhile, in bowl, combine ginger, lime juice, yogurt, mayonnaise, mustard, and curry powder; mix well.

Quick-release pressure. Check for doneness. If necessary, cook under pressure 2 more minutes. When potatoes are done, remove from pot and let cool a few minutes, then peel skin. This is easily done by hand.

Slice potatoes into 1½-inch pieces. Cool.

Toss with celery, bell peppers, and onions, if using. Mix with sauce. Add salt and pepper, and taste, adjusting seasoning if necessary. Chill.

Taro Cake

SERVES 8

I found so many variations of this dish it made my head spin. Most called for rice and tapioca flours, which I thought might be humbug for some folks. So after more poking around, I hit upon a few recipes that utilize regular white flour. The version I put together will appeal to local palates with shiitake mushroom, dried shrimp and the always-ono lup cheong. Incidentally, the pressure cooker is a perfect vehicle for cooking taro, cutting a couple of hours of cooking time down to about 40 minutes. This two-part recipe starts with that process, and then follows with combining the ingredients and steaming the cake in the cooker. In about an hour's time, you've got a hearty taro cake.

2 cups taro (about 1 softball-sized corm), cooked and diced into large cubes
1 cup flour
¾ cup water
2 teaspoons soy sauce
1 tablespoon sherry
2 teaspoons sesame oil
1 tablespoon garlic powder
1 teaspoon salt
2 lup cheong sausage links, thinly sliced
4 large shiitake mushrooms, soaked in water, stems removed and large diced
½ cup dried shrimp, cut into small pieces
¾ cup sliced green onion

First, cook the taro: Wearing gloves, cut off skin of corm. Rinse and cut into several chunks. Place in pressure cooker with ¾ to 1 cup of water. Secure lid, bring to pressure, lower heat and cook about 40 minutes. Quick-release pressure and open lid. Taste taro to ensure it's fully cooked (if your mouth feels itchy, taro is not fully cooked.)

When taro is done, cool slightly then large dice. Set aside.

In large bowl, combine flour and water and mix well. Add soy sauce, sherry, sesame oil, garlic powder, and salt; combine well.

Add taro, lup cheong, mushrooms, shrimp, and green onion. Combine well.

Place taro cake mixture in a 7-inch round casserole dish or glass bowl.

Add 1 cup water to pressure cooker, place trivet in pot, and place foil strips (see page xv) on trivet. These will be used to retrieve bowl from pot when taro cake is cooked. Set dish on foil strips. Tuck in strips, seal lid, bring pot to pressure on high, lower heat, and cook 15 minutes.

Allow natural-pressure release for 5 minutes, then quick-release pressure. Remove dish carefully using foil strips. Cool for a few minutes, then slice taro cake into pieces and serve.

Potstickers

MAKES ABOUT 4 DOZEN

The beauty of this dish is the versatility of the filling. Here, I keep it simple, with a little bit of vegetables to lend some color and texture. Add to the mix some bamboo shoot strips, slivers of carrot, any dark leafy green, or water chestnuts. Even tofu would work. Or go vegetarian with a filling of tofu or other meat substitute and any combo of vegetables. Steaming these in the pressure cooker cuts cooking time nearly in half. As for the accompanying sauce, I include a simple recipe, but use anything you like, from a drizzle of soy sauce to a dot of spicy chili paste. Some folks don't use sauce at all.

1 head kai choy (mustard cabbage), quartered lengthwise and
  thinly sliced
1 pound ground pork or chicken
1 dozen small shrimp, deveined and minced (optional)
4 shiitake mushrooms, soaked, stems removed and small diced
¼ cup sliced chives
1 tablespoon minced or grated ginger
1 teaspoon garlic powder
1 tablespoon sesame oil
1 tablespoon oyster sauce
1½ tablespoons sherry
1 package gyoza wrappers (about 48 pieces)
Won bok or lettuce leaves

Dipping sauce:

½ cup soy sauce
2 tablespoons rice vinegar
1 tablespoon grated ginger
¼ teaspoon sesame oil
½ to 1 teaspoon honey

To make sauce, combine all ingredients, stirring repeatedly until honey is completely incorporated. Set aside.

In bowl, toss kai choy with a sprinkle of salt and let sit 10 minutes. Pour off water released and squeeze vegetable to remove excess water.

Add pork, shrimp if using, shiitake, chives, ginger, garlic, sesame oil, oyster sauce, and sherry. Mix well until pork has pasty consistency.

To wrap potstickers, have small bowl of water and a couple baking sheets handy. On flat surface, place one wrapper and add 1 teaspoon pork mixture to center of wrapper. Dip finger in bowl of water and moisten edge of top half of wrapper. Fold up bottom half and pinch edges together firmly. Place on baking sheet.

Repeat with all wrappers. Do not let potstickers overlap on sheet.

At this point, potstickers can be frozen. Place them carefully in gallon-size resealable bag, separating layers with sheets of parchment paper. Lay flat to freeze, being careful that potstickers do not overlap until frozen.

To cook, add 1 cup water to pressure cooker and place steamer into pot. Line with won bok or lettuce leaves. Place potstickers on leaves. Do not overlap. Cover and bring to pressure, then lower heat and cook 5 minutes.

Quick-release pressure and remove lid. Check if wrapper is nicely cooked, tender but still chewy. If wrapper is still too chewy, place lid on pot but do not seal, turn up heat until water boils and steam until wrappers are tender.

Repeat until all potstickers are cooked.

Cauliflower Casserole

SERVES 8 TO 10

saw a variation of this recipe in a community cookbook and thought an adaptation for the pressure cooker would perfectly illustrate its virtues. The original recipe calls for boiling or blanching the cauliflower. Using the pressure cooker to handle this step saves time and keeps more nutrients in the vegetable. This dish, rich with butter and cheddar cheese, is a perfect addition to any potluck table.

2 medium cauliflower, broken into 2-inch florets
¼ cup butter
5 cloves garlic, minced
2 cups panko
¼ cup plain Greek yogurt
1 teaspoon paprika
2 teaspoons salt
2 cups grated cheddar

Preheat oven to 325°F. Fill pressure cooker with 1 cup water and place stainless-steel steamer basket inside. Pile cauliflower on basket.

Seal lid, bring to pressure, lower heat, and cook 1 minute. Quick-release pressure under running tap. Remove cauliflower to large bowl. Lightly mash; set aside.

In large pan on medium-high heat, melt butter and sauté garlic. When fragrant, add panko, tossing until panko turns golden. Remove from heat and set aside.

In large mixing bowl, combine yogurt, paprika, and salt. Add cauliflower and mix until pieces are coated with yogurt. Add cheese and mix again. Add 1½ cups of panko and toss.

Place cauliflower in greased casserole dish or 9 × 13-inch pan. Top with remaining panko. Bake 40 minutes.

Miso Eggplant

SERVES 4

Our family loves eggplant, and this recipe has long been a favorite way to prepare it. Miso and a generous amount of oil lends heartiness to the veggie, and for vegetarians, it's a perfect main dish. One note of caution: Be sure not to cut the eggplant too thin, or it will turn to mush under pressure. Likewise, pay close attention to the cooking time. Vegetables in general, and eggplant especially, need to treated delicately when pressure cooked.

3 tablespoons white miso
1 cup water
1 teaspoon dashi
½ teaspoon sugar
¼ cup olive oil
1½ teaspoons garlic powder
6 medium Japanese eggplant, sliced into 2½-inch pieces about
   ½-inch thick

In bowl, combine miso, water, dashi, and sugar. Mix well.

Heat oil and garlic powder in pot. Stir-fry eggplant in pot briefly, about 2 minutes. Pour miso mixture over eggplant. Seal lid, bring to pressure on high, lower heat, and cook 1 minute. Quick-release pressure under running tap.

Open lid and check for doneness. If necessary, cover pot loosely with lid and simmer for 5 minutes.

Tofu-Stuffed Aburage
SERVES 4

*C*hef Alyssa Moreau says cone sushi has always been a comfort food, and her vegetarian recipe for stuffed aburage is a great option for adding protein to the diet, since it's filled with tofu rather than rice. Moreau says the morsels can be eaten hot, cold, or at room temperature, making them perfect for snacking or eating on the run. She calls the dish "a power packet of flavors and textures."

1½ packages aburage
¾ cup water

Stuffing:

1 container tofu, drained well
1 (8-ounce) can water chestnuts, chopped
2 tablespoons green onions
2 tablespoons Chinese parsley
6 shiitake mushrooms, soaked, stemmed, and minced
2 tablespoons grated carrot
2 cloves garlic, minced, or 1 teaspoon garlic powder
1 tablespoon ginger, minced
1 tablespoon sesame oil
2 tablespoons soy sauce
Salt, to taste

Sauce:

2 cups vegetable broth or mushroom stock
3 tablespoons soy sauce
2 tablespoons sugar
1 tablespoon oyster sauce
½ teaspoon sesame oil
½ teaspoon salt
2 tablespoons cornstarch mixed with 2 tablespoons water
Chili paste, to taste

Place aburage in pressure cooker with water. Seal lid, bring to pressure on high heat, then quick-release pressure. Do not drain water. Remove aburage from pot, cool, gently squeeze out liquid. Then cut a slit on the diagonal to form a pocket. Set aside.

To make sauce, in another pot, combine ingredients, bring to boil and simmer until thickened. Set aside.

In bowl, mix stuffing ingredients. Stuff into aburage pockets.

Add steamer basket to pressure cooker pot. Place pockets in basket, seal lid, bring to pressure, lower heat, and cook 5 minutes. Quick-release pressure. Remove to dish and pour sauce over pockets.

{ Enter the Entrée }

Local fare has always been diverse. Think stuffed bittermelon versus chicken lūʻau versus miso pork. But today, that variety is expanded even further to encompass the upscale (Braised Abalone with Daikon) and the creative reimagining of classic dishes (Vegetarian Oden). In all cases, preparation in the pressure cooker delivers efficiency and boosted flavor.

Oxtail Stew

SERVES 6

For a couple of years, I worked with Kathleen Freitas of Hawaiian Electric Co. on the "Electric Kitchen" column we run in the Honolulu Star-Advertiser food section every Wednesday. Kathleen is a foodie and avid cook who told me her family loves to use the pressure cooker. This stew is from her grandmother, Connie Kop, who, incidentally, was also a Hawaiian Electric employee. Kathleen said that while oxtail doesn't always appeal to youngsters, this dish is treasured among young and old in her family.

2 yellow onions, peeled and roughly chopped
4 pounds oxtail
2 packets beef stew seasoning mix
1 (14.5-ounce) can Italian-style seasoned diced tomatoes
1 head cabbage, core removed and roughly chopped
5 carrots, peeled and sliced into 2-inch pieces
4 stalks celery, thinly sliced
4 potatoes, peeled and quartered
2 (14.5-ounce) cans beef broth

Spray nonstick cooking spray on bottom of pot and fry onions over medium-high heat until golden brown, 1 to 2 minutes. Add oxtail and brown on each side for 1 to 2 minutes.

Add remaining ingredients, stir well, and seal lid. Bring to pressure on high heat, lower heat, and cook 30 minutes. Remove from heat and allow natural-pressure release for 15 minutes. Quick-release pressure and serve.

FAST

Galbi Jim
(Korean Short Rib and Pear Stew)
SERVES 6

Kathleen Freitas, who regularly pressure cooks her meals at home, shares this recipe, a favorite because she loves the combination of pears with soy sauce and mirin, which produce a mellow sweet-sour flavor. Kathleen chops her pear into cubes because she enjoys the added texture but says you can grate the pear if you like. This allows the fruit to dissolve into the sauce.

2 pounds beef short ribs
5 large dried shiitake mushrooms, soaked, stems removed and thinly sliced
½ Asian pear, peeled, cored and cut into ½-inch cubes
2 carrots, peeled and cut into 1-inch pieces
2 tablespoons mirin
¼ cup soy sauce
1 tablespoon brown sugar
¼ cup thinly sliced green onion
2 cloves garlic, peeled and chopped, or 1 tablespoon garlic powder
Ground black pepper, to taste
1 cup water

Combine all ingredients in pot and mix until incorporated. Seal lid, bring to pressure on high, then lower heat and cook 45 minutes.

Remove from heat and allow natural-pressure release for 15 minutes. Quick-release pressure and serve.

Oriental Steak

SERVES 6

This dish was a childhood favorite, hearty and satisfying. My mother did two variations, one with a brown sauce, the other with tomato sauce. Both used button mushrooms and probably some type of chuck. Here, I use shiitake, which adds great flavor, and flank steak, though any cut will do since the pressure cooker is great for delivering tender meat.

3 pounds flank steak, cut into strips about 3 to 4 inches wide (or any other type of leaner beef cut)
Salt and pepper, to taste
2 tablespoons oil plus more as necessary
1 medium onion, sliced
¼ cup flour
6 large shiitake mushrooms, soaked in 3 cups of water, stemmed and sliced (or 1 cup pre-sliced mushrooms); reserve water

Season beef with salt and pepper. Set aside.

Heat oil in pressure-cooker pot over medium-high and quickly sauté onions. Remove and set aside.

Return pot to burner on medium-high. Dip beef strips in flour, shake off excess, and brown in pot, about 2 to 3 minutes each side. Remove strips as they brown and finish all the pieces.

Return beef to pot, add soaked mushrooms and reserved water, and top with onions. Seal lid, bring pot to pressure, lower heat and cook 25 minutes.

Allow natural-pressure release and remove lid. Skim off fat from top of broth. Test beef for tenderness. Fork should easily penetrate and tear meat. If necessary, cook under pressure another 5 to 10 minutes. Allow natural-pressure release.

Local Style Curry

SERVES 6

This recipe can be whipped up within 30 minutes from start to finish, since cooking time for a beef version is about 16 minutes (plus 10-minute natural-pressure release) or a mere 8 minutes if you use chicken. It's a natural for the weeknight recipe rotation.

1 tablespoon cooking oil
1 onion, chopped
3 pounds beef, cut into 1-inch thick cubes*
2 (14.5-ounce) cans beef or chicken broth
2 bay leaves
¼ cup curry powder
1 tablespoon garlic powder
1½ teaspoons salt
2 large potatoes, cut into 1-inch chunks
2 carrots, cut into 1-inch chunks
3 celery stalks, cut into 2-inch pieces
2 tablespoons cornstarch dissolved in 2 tablespoons water

In pressure cooker pot, heat oil and sauté onions, about 2 minutes. Add beef and brown.

Add broth, bay leaves, curry powder, garlic powder, and salt. Seal lid, bring to pressure on high, lower heat, and cook 12 minutes. Naturally release pressure for 10 minutes, then quick-release if necessary.

Add potatoes, carrots, and celery. Seal lid, bring to pressure, lower heat, and cook another 4 minutes. Remove from heat and quick-release, then open lid and return pot to burner on medium. Curry should be simmering.

Stir cornstarch mixture, then add to curry and stir while thickening. Simmer 5 minutes and serve.

{ * } Beef can be replaced with boneless chicken breast or thighs. Add vegetables along with chicken, then cook at pressure for 4 minutes, plus 4-minute natural release. Quick-release, then proceed with thickening gravy.

Chicken Lū'au

SERVES 6 TO 8

*S*et aside a couple hours at home to make this rich, comforting dish. Most of the hands-on work is cleaning and removing stems from the lū'au leaves (remember to use gloves). After that, it's mostly a waiting game while the leaves cook down. When that's complete, work with just a few more ingredients and you'll have chicken lū'au within 30 minutes.

2 to 2½ pounds lū'au leaves
1½ cups water, divided
1 pound bone-in chicken thighs
1 tablespoon garlic powder
2 teaspoons salt
1 can coconut milk

Wash leaves and remove stems. Chop leaves into manageable size so they can fit inside pressure cooker. Add 1 cup water, seal lid, bring pot to pressure on high heat, then lower heat and cook 50 minutes. Quick-release pressure and taste leaves. If your mouth feels itchy, leaves are not yet thoroughly cooked. Seal lid, return pot to pressure, and cook another 10 minutes.

When leaves are cooked, drain water. Add to pot ½ cup water, chicken, garlic powder, and salt. Seal lid, bring pot to pressure, lower heat, and cook 10 minutes. Remove from heat, allow natural-pressure release for 4 minutes, then quick-release.

Remove chicken thighs. Add coconut milk and stir. Cover with lid but do not seal and simmer 10 to 15 minutes. Meanwhile, shred chicken, adding meat to pot and discarding bones. Stir, taste, and adjust seasoning if necessary.

Chicken Papaya

SERVES 4 TO 6

Having grown up with Japanese-influenced home cooking, I enjoy a squash stir-fry: kabocha with pork or aburage, long squash and chicken. It is the latter that this Filipino dish most reminds me of, but chicken papaya is much more flavorful with its aromatic green papaya and punches of patis and fresh ginger. The dish is cooked in two stages: chicken first, then papaya is added to the pot. Total cooking time is about 30 minutes.

1 tablespoon olive oil
2 pounds bone-in chicken thighs, skin and fat removed
1 onion, large dice
2 cups water
1 (14.5-ounce) can chicken broth
2½ tablespoons patis
2 teaspoons garlic powder
1 finger ginger, peeled and smashed
2 teaspoons salt, or to taste
½ bunch marungay leaves (about 3 cups)
4 pounds green papaya

Heat oil in pot, brown chicken and onions, about 5 minutes.

Add water, broth, patis, garlic powder, ginger, and salt. Mix, seal lid, bring pot to pressure on high, lower heat, and cook 12 minutes.

Meanwhile, rinse marungay, pluck from stalks, and set aside.

Rinse papaya, slice off ends and halve lengthwise. Scoop out seeds, then peel off skin with vegetable peeler. Slice into 2-inch chunks.

Remove pot from heat and quick-release pressure. Add papaya and marungay. Quickly mix, seal lid and bring to pressure again. Lower heat and cook 8 minutes. Quick-release and check papaya for doneness. It should be very tender.

If papaya needs to be cooked further, cook under pressure 2 more minutes, then quick-release pressure.

If you like, remove chicken from pot, shred meat and return to pot, discarding bones. Stir and serve.

Chicken Hekka

SERVES 6

M y mom's chicken hekka was always a welcome sight at the dinner table. It offered a delicious mix of textures and flavors, with its crunchy water chestnuts, chewy udon noodles, flavorful chicken bites, earthy bamboo shoots and tofu cubes touched with the subtle flavor of the dish's "sato-shoyu" (sugar and soy sauce) sauce. So when I decided to put together this collection of local recipes, I knew I had to adapt her dish for the pressure cooker.

1 tablespoon olive oil
6 boneless, skinless chicken thighs, cut into bite-size pieces
1 finger ginger, peeled and crushed
½ (14.5-ounce) can chicken broth
2 teaspoons garlic powder
1 cup soy sauce
½ cup mirin
3 tablespoons sugar
1 block firm tofu, cut into approximately 2-inch chunks and well drained
2 medium onions, sliced in half then in strips
1 bunch watercress, cleaned and sliced into 2-inch lengths
½ bunch green onion, cut into 2-inch lengths
1 (10-ounce) can button mushrooms, drained
1 (8-ounce) can sliced bamboo shoots, drained
1 (8-ounce) can sliced water chestnuts, drained
1 package fresh udon

In pot, heat oil and brown chicken. Add ginger and stir-fry until fragrant. Add broth and garlic powder. Seal lid, and on high heat, bring to pressure, lower heat, and cook 3 minutes.

While chicken is cooking, mix soy sauce, mirin, and sugar.

Quick-release pressure, then add sauce, tofu, onions, watercress, and green onion. Seal lid, bring pot to pressure, then immediately quick-release pressure.

Add mushrooms, bamboo shoots, water chestnuts, and udon. Cover but do not seal lid. Simmer until these items are heated, about 5 to 10 minutes.

Thai Chicken Curry

SERVES 3 TO 4

The rise of the farmers' market has opened up the culinary world for home cooks. Used to be, I'd have to make a special trip to specialty markets to find galangal (a relative of ginger), lemongrass, kaffir leaves and Thai chilies to make this dish. Now, I can find these ingredients, freshly picked, during my weekly jaunt to the neighborhood farmers' market. Honestly, this curry doesn't take lots of time to make in the pan. But cooked in the pressure cooker, it takes more time to slice the ingredients than it does to prepare them, and slicing can be done in advance. That convenience has placed Thai curry on my weeknight dinner rotation.

1 boneless, skinless chicken breast, sliced into ½-inch thick strips
½ cup chicken broth
1 (13.5-ounce) can coconut milk
1½ to 2 tablespoons red curry paste, or to taste
1 finger galangal, peeled and crushed
1 Thai chili, sliced (optional)
4 kaffir leaves, cracked
2 medium eggplant, cut into 2½-inch slices ½-inch thick
½ (8.5-ounce) can bamboo shoots strips (optional)
½ (15-ounce) can baby corn (optional)
½ (8-ounce) can sliced water chestnuts
Salt, to taste

Place chicken and broth in pot. Seal lid, bring to pressure on high, lower heat, and cook 3 minutes. Quick-release pressure.

Meanwhile, in bowl, mix coconut milk, curry paste, galangal, chili, if using, and kaffir.

Add coconut milk mixture and eggplant to pot. Reseal, bring to pressure, lower heat, and cook 1 minute. Quick-release pressure under running tap water.

Add rest of ingredients and salt to taste. Simmer with lid off for several minutes.

Nishime

SERVES 8

For Japanese families, there's no party fare more standard than nishime. Crafting a nishime recipe for the pressure cooker takes some know-how, given that some ingredients are rather delicate for this style of cooking. But leave it to chef Grant Sato to figure it out, then graciously share his expertise.

1 package dried konbu (sold in Asian section of supermarkets)
1 pound gobo, cut into obliques (cut crosswise at an angle)
1 package konnyaku, cut into triangles (available in refrigerated section near fresh tofu)
4 pieces dried shiitake mushrooms, soaked, stemmed and cut into bite-size pieces
⅓ pound fresh hasu (lotus root), peeled and cut into ¼-inch slices
8 cups dashi (Japanese stock, made from powder sold in Asian section of supermarkets)
½ cup soy sauce
½ cup brown sugar
1 pound chicken or pork, cut into 1-inch strips
1 carrot, cut into obliques
1 can bamboo shoots, cut into 1-inch strips
1 pound araimo (Japanese taro), peeled and cut into 1-inch cubes

Soak dried konbu until hydrated and pliable. Tie into 8 knots about 3 inches apart, then cut between knots. Set aside.

In pot, place gobo, konnyaku, shiitake, hasu, dashi, soy sauce, and brown sugar. Seal lid, bring to pressure on high, lower heat and cook 10 minutes.

Quick-release pressure and add meat, carrots, konbu knots, bamboo shoots, and araimo. Simmer uncovered for 15 minutes. Taste and add more soy sauce if necessary.

Ma Po Tofu

SERVES 2 TO 3

This hearty, spicy Chinese comfort food offers loads of flavor with minimal effort. While some recipes call for simmering the tofu in a separate pot while browning the pork, this recipe calls for a quick minute of pressure cooking the tofu at the end, making for a convenient one-pot dish. The most time-consuming aspect of this recipe is mincing the ginger. If your ginger is fibrous and difficult to mince, simply grate it. For more heat, up the cayenne, or eliminate it if you want a more mellow dish.

Sauce:

¼ cup chicken broth
½ tablespoon chili-garlic sauce
½ tablespoon fermented black beans, rinsed and smashed
2 tablespoons soy sauce
Salt, to taste

Tofu and pork mixture:

1½ tablespoon oil
½ pound ground pork
1½ tablespoons minced ginger
2 teaspoons garlic powder
2 tablespoons cooking sherry
1 tablespoon cornstarch dissolved in 1 tablespoon water
1 (20-ounce) block soft tofu, drained and cut into ½-inch cubes
2 teaspoons sesame oil
¼ teaspoon dried cayenne pepper, or to taste
Salt, to taste
½ cup chopped green onion, or to taste
8 ounces (half bag) frozen peas and carrots, thawed (optional)

To make sauce, stir together broth, chili-garlic sauce, black beans, soy sauce and salt. Set aside.

For tofu and pork mixture, heat oil in pressure cooker pot. Add pork and brown, breaking up chunks as it cooks. Add ginger and cook until fragrant, about 2 minutes.

Add garlic powder and sherry and stir. Mix in cornstarch and stir well.

Add tofu and sauce, and stir gently. Seal lid, bring to pressure on high, lower heat, and cook 1 minute. Remove from heat and quick-release pressure.

Remove lid. Add sesame oil, cayenne, salt, green onions, and peas and carrots, if using. Stir gently.

Portuguese Sausage Chili

SERVES 6

Ever since I got my pressure cooker, I've been experimenting with different chili recipes and spices. I've learned that cumin and cinnamon added to chili powder provide a winning depth of flavor. I've concocted this sweeter chili using kabocha, which also adds sweetness and thickness to the sauce, along with some pineapple jelly. Add to the pot spicy Portuguese sausage and it's a perfect match. For more heat, up the chili powder; amp it up further with dried crushed red pepper or cayenne.

1 cup dry black beans
1 cup dry navy beans
4½ cups water, divided
1 tablespoon oil
1 (8- or 10-ounce) Portuguese sausage, casing removed and diced
½ package bacon, sliced crosswise into ½-inch strips, then diced
1 large onion, diced
1 cup kabocha, diced into ½-inch pieces
2 tablespoons pineapple jelly
2 teaspoons salt, or to taste
3 tablespoons chili powder, or to taste
2 tablespoons cumin
¼ teaspoon ground cinnamon
½ teaspoon cayenne pepper or 1 tablespoon dried crushed red
    pepper (optional)
2 (15-ounce) cans tomato sauce
2 (14.5-ounce) cans diced tomatoes

Rinse beans, then place in pressure cooker with 4 cups of water and oil. Seal lid, bring to pressure, lower heat, and cook 22 minutes. Remove pot from heat and allow pressure to re-lease naturally, about 15 more minutes.

Drain beans and set aside.

In pot, fry sausage and drain on paper towel. Set aside.

Fry bacon and onions in pot, then drain on paper towel. Drain out three quarters of oil.

Return bacon and onions to pot. Add remaining water, kabocha, pineapple jelly, salt, and spices. Mix well.

Add tomato sauce and diced tomatoes to pot. Do not stir.

Seal lid, bring pot to pressure, reduce heat, and cook 3 minutes. Quick-release pressure.

Return beans and sausage to the pot and stir. Cover but do not seal lid and simmer 5 to 10 minutes.

Pulled Pork
with Guava Barbecue Sauce

SERVES 8 TO 10

The wonders of guava jelly extend far beyond the canvas of a piece of toast, as this recipe will attest. Its presence in a homemade barbecue sauce lends the necessary sweetness to balance the acidity of vinegar and spiciness of Dijon mustard. Add in some other staples of the pantry and you've got a lively sauce that also works well with pork ribs.

1 cup water
4 to 5 pound pork butt roast

Sauce:

1½ tablespoons dried minced onions
¼ cup water
½ cup ketchup
¼ cup guava jelly
2 tablespoons Dijon mustard
2 tablespoons Worchestershire sauce
2 teaspoons vinegar
1 tablespoon soy sauce
2 teaspoons salt
½ teaspoon garlic powder
Chili pepper flakes, to taste (optional)

Place water and pork in pressure cooker pot. Seal lid, bring to pressure on high, lower heat, and cook 1 hour. Allow natural-pressure release, then check for doneness. Meat should fall apart easily when shredded with a fork. If necessary, cook under pressure another 10 to 15 minutes. When done, drain pork and shred with two forks.

While pork is cooking, mix dried onions with water, and let sit for 10 minutes to hydrate.

In bowl, combine rest of ingredients, whisking together if necessary to incorporate guava jelly. Add onions. Set aside.

When pork is shredded, pour sauce over meat, and mix. Serve on buns, in tortilla wrap, or as pizza topping.

Stuffed Bittermelon with Black Bean Sauce

SERVES 3 TO 4

This classic Chinese favorite is usually enjoyed at a restaurant or a party if you're lucky enough to have an aunty willing to pull it together. It does take time to hollow out the bittermelon pieces, mix the pork filling and stuff it into the vegetable. But in the pressure cooker, it's a short wait from the time the morsels hit the pot to when they're served. And the end product is so perfectly cooked, and the flavors so well infused, it's well worth the effort. You'll probably return to this recipe again and again. I know I have.

2 medium bittermelon, cut crosswise into 2-inch pieces and hollowed out in the center
¾ cup water

Pork filling:

¾ pound ground pork
3 tablespoons minced water chestnuts
3 tablespoons shiitake mushroom, soaked, stemmed, and minced
2 tablespoons minced green onions
½ teaspoon salt
¼ teaspoon pepper
½ teaspoon sesame oil
1 teaspoon soy sauce
1 teaspoon cooking sherry

Black bean sauce:

1½ tablespoons fermented black beans, rinsed and mashed
2 tablespoons minced garlic
2 tablespoons white wine
¾ cup chicken broth
1 tablespoon sesame oil or aji sesame oil
1 tablespoon soy sauce
1 tablespoon oyster sauce

Par-cook bittermelon: Add water to pressure cooker pot, insert steamer basket, place bittermelon pieces in basket. Seal lid, bring to pressure on high heat, lower heat and cook 1 minute. Quick-release pressure. Remove pieces and let cool. Remove basket.

In bowl, mix all ingredients for pork filling and stuff bittermelon pieces. Place in pot.

In small bowl, combine black bean sauce ingredients, mix well, and pour over stuffed bittermelon. Seal lid, bring to pressure, lower heat, and cook 1 minute. Release pressure, open lid, and check if pork filling is cooked. If necessary, cook under pressure another minute. Release pressure, then simmer 5 minutes.

Stuffed Tofu

MAKES 6 STUFFED TOFU

This dish is versatile. Change up the pork filling by adding diced water chestnuts or bamboo shoots. Shrimp is optional as well. The dipping sauce can reflect any flavor palette. Here it is pungent and spicy with chili-garlic paste and ginger, a nice balance to the richness of the stuffed tofu.

1 (14-ounce) firm tofu, cut into 6 pieces about 3 by 1½ inches, and well drained

Pork filling:

½ pound ground pork
3 tablespoons finely chopped shrimp
3 tablespoons finely chopped shiitake
1 teaspoon oyster sauce
1 teaspoon sesame oil
1 teaspoon sugar
2 teaspoons cooking sherry
½ teaspoon salt

Dipping sauce:

2 tablespoons soy sauce
½ teaspoon chili-garlic paste
½ teaspoon sugar
1 teaspoon grated or minced ginger
Green onion, for garnish

Scoop out tofu from center of each piece to make a well, using tea-spoon. Set aside.

In bowl, combine pork with shrimp, shiitake, oyster sauce, sesame oil, sugar, sherry, and salt. Mix thoroughly.

Divide pork mixture among 6 tofu pieces (approximately 2 table-spoons per piece) and stuff tofu.

Fill pressure cooker with 1 cup of water and place steamer inside pot. Line steamer with foil and place stuffed tofu on top. Seal lid and bring pot to pressure on high. Lower heat and cook 4 to 5 minutes.

Meanwhile, make dipping sauce. Combine soy sauce, chili-garlic paste, sugar, and ginger. Set aside.

When tofu is cooked, remove pot from heat and quick-release pressure. Carefully remove tofu from steamer with tongs and spatula.

Garnish with green onion. Serve with dipping sauce.

Sari Sari

SERVES 4

Cook this delicious, nutritious dish in stages. First, prepare the delicate veggies, followed by more hardy ones. Then, use the cooker as a standard pot to sauté and simmer. The final product is a classic Filipino dish made convenient with a modern appliance.

2-inch piece ginger, peeled and smashed
2 to 3 Japanese eggplant, sliced into 2½ inch pieces about ½-inch thick
1 large onion, wedged
1 cup water, divided
1 small bunch long beans, sliced into 2½ inch pieces
1½ dozen okra, sliced into 1½ inch pieces
⅓ small kabocha, sliced into 2-inch chunks
2 large tomatoes, sliced into 2-inch chunks
1 tablespoon olive oil
3 to 4 cloves garlic, crushed
1½ to 2 cups lechon or Chinese roast pork, sliced into 1-inch pieces (optional)
2 tablespoons patis (fish sauce)
1½ tablespoons tomato paste
Salt, to taste

Place ginger, eggplant, onion and ½ cup water in pot. Seal lid, bring to pressure on high, then immediately quick-release under running tap. Remove contents from pot; set aside.

Return ginger to pot with beans, okra, kabocha, tomatoes, and remaining water. Seal lid, bring to pressure on high, lower heat, and cook 1 minute. Quick-release pressure under running tap. Remove contents from pot; set aside.

In pot on high, heat oil and garlic. Reduce heat to medium-low, add lechon and sauté 2 minutes. Return veggies to pot. Add patis and tomato paste, and stir. Add salt. Cover pot but don't seal. Simmer 10 minutes.

Black Bean Spare Ribs

SERVES 4

This recipe comes courtesy of Hawaiian Electric employee Kathleen Freitas, an avid fan of the pressure cooker. It was passed on to her from mother-daughter cooking team Stephanie and Briana Ackerman (Briana is a colleague) for a lineup of Chinese New Year recipes that Hawaiian Electric was sharing with the community. It quickly became one of Freitas' favorites.

¼ cup plus 2 tablespoons black bean and garlic paste (available in the Asian food section of most supermarkets)
2 tablespoons brown sugar
¼ cup water
4 to 5 slices ginger, peeled and cut into 2-inch pieces and crushed
½ cup green onions, finely chopped
¼ cup Chinese parsley, finely chopped
1 tablespoon sesame oil
3 tablespoons flour or tapioca starch
2 pounds pork spare ribs, cut into 1½- to 2-inch pieces

In large bowl, combine all ingredients except flour and spare ribs. Set aside.

Spray nonstick cooking spray on the bottom of pot and fry floured spare ribs over medium-high heat for 1 to 2 minutes on each side until golden brown.

Add black-bean sauce and seal lid, bring to pressure on high, reduce heat, and cook 30 minutes. Remove from heat and allow natural-pressure release for 15 minutes.

Quick-release pressure and serve.

Miso Pork

SERVES 6 TO 8

There's such great return for such little effort from this recipe for a local classic. The flavor is incredible, and because the pressure cooker delivers so quickly, it's easy to pull off this roast for a weeknight dinner. I used a combo of red and white miso because the red offers an earthy flavor, while the white contributes a mellower sweetness. But feel free to use just one type. Be creative with leftovers: fill burritos and quesadillas, top pizzas, shred and top with pickles for sliders, or cube meat and stir-fry with veggies.

5 pounds pork butt, cut into quarters
½ cup white miso
¼ cup red miso
¾ cup soy sauce
½ cup brown sugar
1 finger ginger, peeled and crushed
2 teaspoons garlic powder
¼ cup sake

Add ½ cup water to pot.

Place pork in pot.

Combine miso, soy sauce, sugar, ginger, garlic powder, and sake. Mix, then pour over pork.

Seal lid, and on high heat bring to pressure. Lower heat and cook 40 minutes. Allow natural-pressure release, then check tenderness of pork. It should be soft enough to tear with a fork. If necessary, cook under pressure another 10 minutes.

If you like, finish off the roast in the broiler to char the miso sauce. Broil 3 to 5 minutes.

Kālua Pig

SERVES 8

My first attempt at pressure cooking was executing this recipe, posted on the Tasty Island food blog by Pomai Souza. The post chronicled Souza's misadventures in arriving at a successful kālua pig recipe for the pressure cooker. (Actually, it's more procedure than recipe.) I followed Souza's directives and produced a wonderfully moist, flavorful, and fool-proof kālua pig, all within 2 hours. Here, I pass on Souza's knowledge with my approximations for a formal recipe. Adjust as you see fit. For visuals and his take on the process, visit Souza's blog at http://tastyislandhawaii.com/2011/04/03/pressure-cooked-kalua-pig/

6 ti leaves, stems removed
5-pound pork butt with a generous fat cap
⅛ cup Hawaiian salt, or to taste
3 tablespoons liquid smoke, or to taste
2 cups water

Wash ti leaves and set aside to dry.

Deeply score pork and rub in salt and liquid smoke on each side of roast. Place into pressure cooker pot fat side up. Pour water into side of pot. Line sides of pot and cover top of roast with more ti leaves. (Do not line bottom of pot with leaves—it will scorch.)

Seal lid, bring to pressure on high, lower heat and cook 1½ hours. Turn off heat and leave on burner. Allow natural-pressure release, about 30 minutes.

Release lid and check for doneness. Pork should fall apart and shred easily with a fork. If necessary, cook under pressure an additional 15 minutes. Allow natural-pressure release. Release lid and taste, adjusting seasoning as necessary.

Remove pork and shred. Reserve liquid in pot and pour over kālua pig when serving to enhance juiciness.

Bean Casserole

SERVES 6

This hearty vegetarian dish shows off one of the best uses of the pressure cooker: preparing dried beans, which cuts down cooking time substantially. For general directions on cooking beans, see page 130. I've selected cooking garbanzo, kidney, and black beans, but they can be replaced with any favorite bean. Just adjust cooking times accordingly.

1 cup dried garbanzo beans
1 cup dried kidney beans
1 cup dried black beans
10 cups water, divided
1 tablespoon oil
1½ cups grated cheese

Sauce:

1 tablespoon olive oil
1 onion, chopped
5 cloves garlic, minced
3 ounces (½ can) tomato paste
½ cup water
1 (14.5-ounce) can diced tomatoes
½ cup guava jelly
3 tablespoons brown sugar
1 tablespoon mustard
1 tablespoon soy sauce
1 teaspoon salt

Pressure cook beans: To pot, add garbanzo beans, 9 cups water, and oil. Seal lid, bring to pressure on high heat, lower heat, and cook 10 minutes. Quick-release pressure.

Add kidney beans, bring to pressure, lower heat, and cook 2 minutes. Quick-release pressure. Add black beans and another cup of water. Bring to pressure, lower heat, and cook 21 minutes. When done, allow natural-pressure release, about 15 minutes. Drain beans well. Set aside.

FAST

Preheat oven to 400°F.

To make sauce, in pan, heat oil and sauté onions and garlic, about 5 minutes. Remove from heat.

In large bowl, incorporate tomato paste and water. Add diced tomatoes, guava jelly, sugar, mustard, soy sauce, and salt. Add onions and garlic and mix well.

Add beans to bowl and combine with sauce.

Grease casserole dish and add beans. Bake 30 minutes uncovered, or until casserole is heated through. Remove casserole, top with grated cheese, and return to oven for 3 to 5 minutes to melt cheese.

Braised Abalone with Daikon

SERVES 4

This dish features fresh abalone, a wonderful product raised on Hawai'i island that's readily used by chefs throughout the state and made available to the public at farmers' markets and some supermarkets. Also, purchase the abalone online at www.bigislandabalone. com. This tasty recipe comes courtesy of Kapi'olani Community College chef/instructor Grant Sato, who coaches the school's student culinary competition team each year. The dish was part of the lineup in last year's American Culinary Federation student regional competition.

1 pound Big Island Abalone, size SS, in shell
1 cup small-diced daikon
4 cups dashi
2 tablespoons soy sauce
1 tablespoon mirin

Place all ingredients in pressure cooker pot. Seal lid, bring to pressure on high, lower heat, and cook 28 minutes.

Quick-release pressure and serve abalone with daikon and broth.

Salmon with Vegetables
SERVES 6

One of the fastest and easiest ways to prepare fish in a pressure cooker is in a single serving-size packet of foil. Cooking is quick and clean up even faster. Try this with salmon. There are endless local preparations for salmon, among them this one, of vegetables tossed with a little mayonnaise and a touch of lemon juice, then spread over the fish. Other recipes mix the mayo with furikake and wasabi, or with Japanese-style pickled vegetables.

1 small zucchini, cut into quarters lengthwise, then into ½-inch pieces
½ small carrot, sliced into bite-size pieces about ¼-inch thick
3 red potatoes, halved and cut in ¼-inch slices
1 small onion, large dice
2 tablespoons mayonnaise
Salt and pepper, to taste
4 (6-ounce) salmon fillets, ½ to 1-inch thick
Squeeze lemon juice

In medium bowl, combine vegetables with mayonnaise, salt, and pepper. Mix well. Set aside.

Cut 6 heavy-duty aluminum foil sheets about 10 × 10 inches in size.

Place 1 piece fish on foil and cover with vegetables. Seal packet tightly. Repeat with rest of fish and vegetables.

Pour 1 cup of water into pot and insert steamer. Place fish packets on steamer, stacking evenly around pot.

Seal lid and bring to pressure on high. Lower heat and cook 8 to 10 minutes. Quick-release after 8 minutes and carefully remove 1 packet. Carefully open packet and check for doneness. If fish or vegetables aren't fully cooked, close packet tightly and pressure cook 2 more minutes. Quick-release and carefully remove packets. When serving, add quick squeeze of lemon juice.

Tofu Casserole

SERVES 6

This rich, almost custardy dish has become my new comfort food. It's versatile—feel free to replace pork and shrimp with bite-size pieces of chicken, and omit or add any veggies that you like. Remember, however, that shiitake adds lots of flavor, so it's an ingredient that goes a long way. A note: drain tofu as thoroughly as possible. Even with hours-long draining in the refrigerator, my cooked casserole had excessive liquid. I drained off about half of it, but as the liquid was well flavored, I kept the rest to pour over my rice when I ate the dish.

¼ pound ground pork
¼ pound shrimp, large diced
3 shiitake mushrooms, soaked, stems removed and large diced
1 cup sliced green onion
1 medium carrot, julienned
4 ounces (½ can) bamboo shoot strips
4 ounces (½ can) sliced water chestnuts, cut into thirds
1 egg
¼ cup panko
1 tablespoon grated or minced ginger
1½ teaspoons sesame oil
2 teaspoons garlic powder
1 teaspoon salt
Pepper, to taste
1 (20-ounce) block soft tofu, crumbled by hand into medium
    chunks and well drained

In large bowl, combine everything but tofu and mix well. Add tofu and gently combine. Transfer to 7-inch round glass bowl or casserole dish.

Fill pot with 1 cup water. Place trivet in pot. Place foil strips on trivet for retrieving dish later when casserole is cooked. To construct strips, see page xv. Tuck the ends into the pot, cover, and seal lid.

Bring pot to pressure on high, lower heat, and cook 15 minutes. Quick-release pressure. Untuck foil strips and carefully hoist dish from pot. There will be excess liquid. Drain if desired, or serve with casserole.

FAST

Vegetarian Oden with Black Sesame Drizzle

SERVES 4 TO 6

{ *C*hef Alyssa Moreau sometimes recommends that her vegetarian dishes be supplemented with meat if they're being served to folks who eat animal products. But the flavors in this dish are so complete, there really isn't any need for meat. "It's a meal within itself," she says. A sesame sauce, based on a recipe by well-known vegan chef Mark Reinfeld, accompanies Moreau's tasty dish. }

½ cup onion
1 tablespoon light oil
¼ cup mirin
1 cup daikon, peeled and cut into obliques (crosswise at an angle)
1 cup lotus, peeled and cut into ¼-inch slices
1 cup carrot, peeled and cut into obliques (crosswise at an angle)
½ cup gobo, peeled and cut into ¼-inch slices
1 cup parsnip, peeled cut into obliques (crosswise at an angle)
1-inch piece konbu
1 cup fresh shiitake, sliced thin
5 cups water
1 package age tofu (fried tofu)*
2 to 4 tablespoons ginger, grated for juice
2 tablespoons soy sauce
1 tablespoon rice vinegar
2 tablespoons arrowroot or cornstarch, dissolved in ¼ cup cold water
¼ cup sliced green onion
Salt, to taste

Sauté onion in oil until translucent.

Add mirin and stir to scrape up browned bits and simmer to reduce and concentrate flavors, about 3 minutes. Add root vegetables, konbu, shiitake, and water to cover, bring up to pressure and cook 2 to 3 minutes. Chop konbu into smaller pieces and return to pot. Add tofu.

While stew cooks, grate and squeeze out juice of ginger using cheesecloth.

Remove pot from heat, quick-release pressure. Open pot and carefully retrieve konbu. Chop into small pieces and return to pot. Add tofu. Add soy sauce, vinegar, and ginger juice. Thicken with arrowroot mixture and stir in green onions. Season with salt to taste. Serve with Black Sesame Sauce (recipe below).

{ * NOTE } To remove excess oil from age tofu, pressure cook in a few cups of water for 2 minutes then quick-release and drain.

Black Sesame Sauce

¼ cup black sesame seeds
½ cup water
1 tablespoon rice vinegar
1 tablespoon soy sauce
⅓ cup safflower or other light oil
1 tablespoon honey or sugar
1 tablespoon mirin
½ teaspoon chili flakes
1 teaspoon sesame oil
¼ teaspoon salt

Combine ingredients in blender and blend well.

Warm on low heat, and serve on side with oden.

Opah with Black Bean Sauce
SERVES 6

H ere's another foil-packet fish preparation. This time a classic Chinese black bean and ginger sauce is perfectly paired with opah, a rich, oily fish. If you can't get your hands on opah, try tilapia, a versatile fish that's usually readily available.

1½-pound opah fillet
Salt and pepper, to taste
3 tablespoons fermented black beans, rinsed and smashed
3 large cloves garlic, minced
3 tablespoons white wine
1½ tablespoons sugar
1 finger ginger, julienned
2 stalks green onion, sliced diagonally

Cut 6 heavy-duty aluminum foil sheets about 10 × 10 inches in size.

Cut fillet into 6 pieces. Season each with salt and pepper.

Mix black bean with garlic, wine, and sugar.

Place 1 piece fish on foil and spoon about ½ tablespoon black bean sauce on fillet. Top with sprinkling of ginger and green onion. Seal packet tightly.

Repeat with rest of fish.

Pour 1 cup of water into pressure cooker pot and insert steamer. Place fish packets on steamer, stacking evenly around pot.

Seal lid and bring to pressure on high, lower heat, and cook 8 minutes. Quick-release pressure and carefully remove packets.

Asparagus Risotto

SERVES 4 TO 6

*V*egetarian chef and pressure cooker expert Alyssa Moreau says risotto is perfect for the pressure cooker. On the stove, the rice takes a long while to cook and requires constant attention, but in this case, the total cooking time invested is close to just 10 minutes, in the sealed pot. This is among Moreau's favorite recipes, which she calls versatile and delicious, with its layers of flavors.

2 to 3 tablespoons olive oil, divided
2 tablespoons finely sliced onions or shallots
½ cup sliced cremini or shiitake mushrooms
1½ teaspoons garlic powder
1 cup arborio rice
5 cups vegetable broth or water
1 cup sliced asparagus spears
1 to 2 tablespoons fresh lemon juice
Lemon zest
¼ cup fresh parsley, green onion, or chives
Salt and pepper, to taste
Parmesan cheese (optional)

Sauté shallots in the oil for 2 minutes, then add mushrooms and stir until they begin to brown and release their juices. Add garlic powder and rice and stir well to coat. Add broth and bring to boil. Seal lid, bring to pressure, lower heat, and cook 6 minutes.

Meanwhile, in small pan, sauté asparagus in a bit of olive oil until tender but still crisp. Set aside.

Quick-release risotto. Cool a few minutes then add asparagus, lemon juice, zest, and parsley. Season with salt and pepper. Add Parmesan if using.

{ NOTE } Rice may be soupy just after cooking but extra liquid will be absorbed.

{ Desserts & Snacks }

D on't make the mistake of disregarding the pressure cooker for producing a diverse lineup of desserts and snacks. In less time than it will take you to assemble, measure and mix the ingredients, you can cook the vibrant sauce for an ono prune mui. Boiled peanuts are a breeze as well, with cooking time cut from the traditional hours of cooking to just 45 minutes. Bread pudding, rice pudding and puto are a snap as well.

Jasmine Rice Pudding

SERVES 6 TO 8

T he charm of this homey dessert is not only that it's versatile—it can be subtle and creamy or livened up with bits of flavorful dried fruit—but it requires very little effort for a pudding dish. Like most pressure cooker recipes, it overdelivers for the effort expended.

2½ cups water
1 cup jasmine rice
1 tablespoon butter
¼ teaspoon salt
1 (13.5-ounce) can coconut milk
⅓ cup brown sugar
Dried fruit such as cranberries or apricots; larger fruit should be slivered or diced (optional)
1 teaspoon vanilla
1 teaspoon cinnamon
¼ teaspoon nutmeg
¼ teaspoon allspice
Fresh fruit, sliced into small bites (optional)

Combine water, rice, butter, and salt in pressure cooker pot. Seal lid, bring to pressure on high, lower heat, and cook 8 minutes. Quick-release pressure under running tap.

Release lid and return pot to medium-high heat, and add coconut milk, sugar, and dried fruit if using. Bring to boil, stirring, then simmer uncovered about 4 to 6 minutes until consistency is like loose oatmeal. Add vanilla, spices, and fresh fruit if using.

Sweet Bread Pudding
SERVES 6 TO 8

This luscious dessert uses two local favorites, sweet bread and macadamia nuts, though you can swap them for any other type of bread or nut, and a variety of add-ins, including dried fruit or chocolate chips. The dessert is cooked in a 7-inch round glass bowl or casserole dish, which is placed on a trivet and foil strips. For details on this technique, see page xv.

½ cup sugar
1 tablespoon cinnamon
5 tablespoons butter, softened
8 to 12 slices sweet bread, cut into 2 x 4-inch pieces
3 large eggs
1½ cup half-and-half
⅓ cup brown sugar
⅛ teaspoon salt
Diced macadamia nuts, for topping (optional)

In small bowl, combine sugar and cinnamon. Set aside.

Using some butter, grease inside and sides of glass bowl or casserole dish. Set aside.

Butter pieces of bread. Set aside.

In bowl, lightly whisk eggs. Whisk in half-and-half, brown sugar, and salt.

Coat bottom of casserole with ¼ cup egg mixture. Place 4 to 6 pieces of bread into bowl. Pour about a third of egg mixture over bread. Sprinkle with cinnamon/sugar mixture.

Layer with more bread, more egg mixture and follow again with cinnamon/sugar. Repeat once more.

Fill pressure cooker with 2 cups water and place trivet inside pot.

Place foil strips on trivet and put dish of bread pudding on top of strips. Secure lid, bring to pressure on high, and lower heat. Cook 20 to 25 minutes, depending on how much bread is packed into dish.

Remove pot from heat, allow pressure to come down naturally, about 10 minutes. Remove dish from pot using foil strips. Top with macadamia nuts.

If you want, you can brown the top of the bread pudding in a 350°F oven 5 to 10 minutes.

Puto
SERVES 12

This Filipino steamed cake is usually served as mini cupcakes, but in the pressure cooker it's more practical to prepare in a 7-inch round casserole that fits nicely in the pot. There are countless versions of puto, some involving white flour and others using rice, and many incorporating coconut milk. This one is distinct in that it uses Bisquick, which produces a yellow cake rather than one that's snowy white. Though it may not look like classic puto, this version is nothing short of delicious and well worth the quick work it takes to make. It comes courtesy of family friends Joe and Sally Aguinaldo, whose Filipino dishes always delight.

1¼ cups Bisquick
6 ounces (½ of 12-ounce can) evaporated milk
3½ ounces (¼ of 14-ounce can) sweetened condensed milk
¼ cup sugar
1 egg

Fill pressure cooker with 1 cup of water and insert trivet. Insert foil strips for removing casserole dish (see page xv). Grease 7-inch round casserole dish.

In bowl, whisk all ingredients together. Pour into casserole. Place casserole into pot on top of foil strips. Place dish on top of the strips. Tuck the ends of the strips into the pot, cover, and seal. On high heat, bring pot to pressure, then lower heat and steam puto for 16 minutes.

Quick-release pressure, open lid, and, using foil strips, remove casserole from pot. Test for doneness by inserting toothpick into center of puto; if it comes out clean, puto is done. If not, place foil strips and casserole back into pot, seal lid, bring pot to pressure, lower heat, and cook up to 3 additional minutes.

Remove casserole from pot, test for doneness. If thoroughly steamed, let puto cool for 20 minutes or so, then slice into 12 pieces and serve.

Prune Mui

MAKES ABOUT 4 CUPS

When I tested this recipe, I added a small handful of li hing mui to the sauce before cooking, in hopes it would add some punch. After it was done, I tossed the sauce with the rest of the ingredients, tasted a prune—and cringed. The sauce tasted almost bitter with li hing flavor. I chalked it up as a learning experience and planned to retest the recipe again. But in the five days that the mui was set aside to merge and absorb flavors, the sharpness of the li hing assimilated nicely with the other elements for an assertive, yet rounded sauce. Success!

1 (10-ounce) package pitted prunes
1 (6-ounce) package dried apricots
4 ounces dried mango (about ½ medium package), sliced into thin strips
2 ounces dried cranberries (about ½ small package)
2 ounces lemon peel (about ½ small package), sliced into strips
2 ounces seedless li hing mui (about ½ small package), sliced in half

Sauce:

½ cup brown sugar
1 tablespoon rock salt
1 tablespoon cooking sherry, whiskey or rum
⅓ teaspoon Chinese five-spice powder
4 whole cloves
½ cup fresh lemon juice
Small handful seedless li hing mui

To make sauce, combine all ingredients. Place in pressure cooker, seal lid, and bring to pressure on high. Lower pressure and cook 6 minutes. Remove from heat, quick-release pressure, and cool.

Add dried fruit and crack seed, stir well.

Place in container and store on cool counter for 4 to 5 days, inverting container daily to redistribute sauce.

Chinese Boiled Peanuts

SERVES 4

Star-Advertiser *reader Dorinda Won, an engineer from Alewa Heights, says she spent most of her life avoiding kitchen duty. But these days, she's taken to "dabbling" in cooking and baking, searching the Internet for interesting recipes and then creating her own version. That's how she came up with an original recipe for boiled peanuts that combines cinnamon with anise and cloves for a great aromatic backdrop, and it's become a family favorite. This adapted version is just a tad saltier.*

1 pound raw peanuts in shell
¼ cup dark soy sauce
3 tablespoons sugar
⅛ cup salt
1 (3-inch) stick cinnamon
2 star anise
5 cloves

Wash peanuts then soak in clean water for 30 minutes. Drain.

Place in pressure cooker with remaining ingredients. Add enough water to cover. Seal lid, bring to pressure on high heat, lower heat, and cook 45 minutes.

Quick-release pressure and check for doneness. If necessary, cook another 2 to 5 minutes. Quick-release pressure and let cool in pot. Drain liquid and serve.

SLOW RECIPES

FOR THE SLOW COOKER

{ The Soup Pot }

Soups are an easy first dish for the slow cooker novice. They're simple: Let a few ingredients swim around in a lot of liquid for a long time. The same principle applies whether you're using a pot on the stove or your slow cooker. Just keep in mind that with slow cooking, liquids don't reduce, so flavors don't become concentrated the way they do on the stove. Compensate with spices and other flavor-boosters and you'll learn to love your Crock-Pot soups.

Making Stock

If you do nothing else with your slow cooker, use it to make stock. Few cooking projects are easier or more rewarding, and the end results are both economical and endlessly useful.

In many cases you can start with something you would normally throw away—the bones from a turkey, chicken, or ham. Are you a devotee of the rotisserie chicken from Costco? After you're done with one, throw the carcass into your slow cooker, cover with water, and let it cook overnight. In the morning you'll have two quarts of a stock so flavorful you can sip it as is.

What do you do with it? Remove the bones, strain, and skim the fat. If there's a lot of meat, remove it from the bones to stir into the soup you're going to make soon. If you don't need the stock right away, freeze it in two-cup quantities. Those plastic tubs that margarine or sour cream come in are perfect containers. Sealable plastic bags also work well and are easy to stack in the freezer. Any time you have a recipe that calls for canned stock or broth, pull out one of these instead. It's easy and practically free, plus you can avoid all the extra sodium found in canned broths. Some people freeze stock in ice cube trays, then they have two-tablespoon quantities of stock handy for stir-fries.

Anything you eat that has bones can be the starting point for great stock, from roast duck to baby back ribs to pork or lamb chops. If your recipe for grilled chicken wings directs you to cut off the wing tips, don't discard them, save them for stock. Throw the bones in the freezer until you have enough for a pot. There doesn't have to be much meat on the bones. Slow cooking draws flavor from the cartilage and connective tissue in the bones; collagen in the connective tissue is converted into gelatin and thickens the liquid.

In many restaurant kitchens, the stock pot is kept at a low simmer day and night. A slow cooker provides the same function left to its own devices for 12 hours or so, and you never have to worry about boil-over.

continued on the next page

No leftover bones? Check the clearance meat sections at supermarkets for beef soup bones, turkey necks or wings, ham or beef shanks. Once I came across a package of duck necks—greatest find ever.

A wonderful seafood broth (it's broth when you don't use bones; stock when you do) can be made with the heads and shells of shrimp, or with fish heads. Cooking time will be three to four hours. Add some clam juice, if you want.

For vegetable broth use a mixture of celery, onions, carrots, and several cloves of garlic. For added depth, cruciferous vegetables—cauliflower, cabbage, broccoli—can be added. Fresh herbs and peppercorns are optional. You can roast the vegetables in the oven or brown them in oil on the stovetop first, if you want to go through the trouble. Slow-cook on low eight hours or overnight.

Use your stock or broth in your favorite soup recipe, in the slow cooker or on the stovetop. A few of my favorites follow on the next few pages.

Creamy Curried Butternut Soup

SERVES 8

*D*espite the coconut milk and the creamy texture it creates, this is a light soup that can be made entirely vegan. It's a nice break from the often heavy, meaty dishes typical of slow cooking.

2-pound butternut squash, cut in 8 pieces, peeled and seeded
2 cups vegetable or chicken broth or stock
1 cup diced onion
4 cloves garlic, smashed and minced
2 tablespoons grated ginger, with juice
1 (4-ounce) can coconut milk
1 to 2 tablespoons Thai red curry paste (available in Asian section
   of most supermarkets)
1 tablespoon lime juice
½ cup chopped cilantro

Combine squash, broth, onion, garlic, and ginger in 6- or 7-quart slow cooker. Cook on low 6 hours, until squash is very tender. Use an immersion wand to purée soup in the crock, or mash with a potato masher.

Stir in coconut milk, curry paste, and lime juice. Taste, adding more curry paste or lime if desired. Let cook another 30 minutes to heat through. Serve garnished with cilantro.

{ VARIATIONS } This soup can be made with many types of vegetables. Cauliflower, broccoli, carrots, or a small pumpkin such as kabocha would work well. So would potatoes—russet or sweet. To add protein, stir in some shredded cooked chicken at the end, or raw shrimp (it will cook in the residual heat). Evaporated milk may be swapped for the coconut milk for those who don't like coconut.

Pho Made Easy

SERVES 8

Pho, that deeply flavored Vietnamese comfort soup, was a dish I always thought best left to professionals. Most traditional recipes involve tons of ingredients, hours of prep, and more hours of long, slow cooking. The slow cooker simplifies all that, as the low heat lets the flavors intensify, allowing you to skip such steps as roasting bones or vegetables for the broth.

2 pounds chuck roast
1 teaspoon EACH salt and pepper
8 ounces dry wide rice noodles

Broth:

4 whole cloves
4 whole star anise
1 cinnamon stick
1 stalk lemongrass, outer skin and tough upper stalk removed
2 cups minced onions
6 cloves garlic, minced
4 cups chicken stock
4 cups beef stock
2 cups water
¼ cup fish sauce
2 tablespoons soy sauce
2 tablespoons sugar

Garnishes:

Bean sprouts, basil leaves, lime wedges, Thai hot chili sauce

Wrap cloves, star anise and cinnamon stick in a cheesecloth pouch or place in tea infuser (you may have to break cinnamon stick).

Mince lemongrass. Place in 6-quart slow cooker with spice pouch and remaining broth ingredients.

Place beef in slow cooker. Cook on low about 9 hours, or until meat is very tender. Remove from crock and shred, removing any gristle. Discard spice pouch. Skim fat from broth. Add noodles to broth and cook about 15 minutes, until tender, but don't let them get mushy. Return meat to pot and turn off pot. Let diners garnish their bowls as desired.

{ NOTE } If you expect to have leftovers, it is best to cook noodles separately. Make fresh noodles when you serve the leftover soup.

Slow-Cooked Jook

SERVES 8 TO 10

n many homes, jook is the classic day-after-Thanksgiving meal, made with the bones of the turkey. It is also the go-to comfort food during flu season, after a hospital stay or when someone in the house is just feeling blue.

1 leftover turkey carcass or 1 to 2 chicken carcasses
6 to 8 cups water
1 piece chung choi (Chinese salted turnip, available in Asian markets and some supermarkets, or substitute 1 teaspoon salt)
1½ cups uncooked rice, washed
2-inch piece ginger, crushed
1 teaspoon soy sauce, or more as needed

Optional add-ins:

1 cup raw peanuts
1 cup sliced shiitake mushrooms (soak dry mushrooms in hot water, then slice)

Optional condiments:

Shredded lettuce
Cilantro leaves
Minced pickled vegetables such as takuwan or sambaizuke

continued on the next page

Place chicken or turkey carcass into slow cooker; add water until barely covered. Cook on low at least 4 hours, or let it go overnight.

Strain stock, skim fat, and remove meat from bones. Return stock to pot and refrigerate chicken or turkey meat.

Soak chung choi in water until soft, then rinse and chop. Add to stock with rice and ginger, plus peanuts, if using. Cook on low about 4 hours, until rice is soft (can be cooked longer or held on warm several hours). If using shiitake mushrooms, add in last hour of cooking. Taste broth and add soy sauce if needed. Stir in cooked chicken or turkey.

{ EXPRESS VERSION } If you don't have time to precook your broth, just throw everything into the pot at once. Many people will do this on Thanksgiving night, using their turkey carcass, and wake up to jook the next morning. You will need to fish the bones out from amid the soft-cooked rice.

{ NO BONES? } Follow the same procedure using chicken parts such as a couple of leg quarters or 3 to 4 thighs. You may have more shredded chicken than you need; save the extra to make a salad or sandwiches.

{ Veggies & Sides }

A nd don't discount the slow cooker for making side dishes. Because slow cooking involves such an investment in time, we tend to think of it as useful for main dishes only. If something's going to take six-hours-plus to come to fruition it had better be the main act, right?

There are times when a hearty vegetable dish or a nice stuffing will help round out a meal when the entree is being baked, stir-fried, roasted, or grilled. The fact that it can be cooking away while you shop, clean up and/or prep the main dish is a bonus.

Thanksgiving Side Dishes

The slow cooker can be your best friend at Thanksgiving, cooking up a nice side dish while your oven is busy with the turkey, your stovetop is occupied with four other things, and you're cleaning the house. Or napping.

Many traditional holiday dishes adapt well to slow cooking. Root vegetables and squashes, cranberries, and deep, dark greens all can cook unattended, emerging when your guests do. Some simple ideas:

Cranberry sauce:

Start with 2 bags (24 ounces) of raw berries. Add 2 cups of water (or red wine for extra zoom) and 3 cups of sugar (throw in a cinnamon stick if you have one). Cook on low about 4 hours, until berries burst. Customize with orange slices, raisins, nuts, citrus peel, or whatever else you like. Make it a few days early to reduce stress on Thanksgiving.

Dark greens:

Place 2 pounds of chard, kale, collards, even lūʻau leaves in the crock with 4 cups chicken or vegetable broth (or use 4 cups water and tuck in a ham hock); cook on low 8 to 10 hours, until very tender. Chopped onions and garlic may also be added. After cooking, drain and chop leaves. Dress with vinegar, lemon juice, or hot sauce.

Potatoes, mashed:

For 3 pounds peeled, cubed Yukon Gold potatoes, add 1½ cups water; cook on low 4 to 6 hours, until soft. Drain, then mash and add milk, butter, and seasonings as you like. Do the mashing in the crock, then hold the potatoes on the warm setting until dinner.

Potatoes, roasted:

This works for any type of potato, from russet to sweet. Scrub potatoes and pile into pot; cook on low about 8 hours (sweet potatoes will cook faster; very large russets might take 10 hours). If possible, rearrange potatoes once during cooking. Skins may be rubbed with oil and coarse salt if you like.

Pumpkin or squash:

Toss wedges with olive oil, salt and pepper; cook on low 4 to 6 hours, until tender but not too soft. Soy sauce or butter and brown sugar can be used instead of salt and pepper. To make a purée, cook until very soft, then mash with butter and cream.

Slow-Simmered Kabocha

Kabocha, sometimes called Japanese pumpkin, is my favorite vegetable to make in the slow cooker, so easily done it's just silly. This recipe uses homemade dashi, the making of which is a good basic technique to know. If you don't want to bother, though, use 2 cups chicken or vegetable broth.

Serve it as a side dish or make it a vegetarian meal with a serving of rice. One serving is incredibly low in calories and other bad things.

1 small kabocha squash, about 2 pounds
2 tablespoons mirin
1 tablespoon sugar
1 tablespoon soy sauce
1 teaspoon slivered ginger

Dashi

2-inch square piece konbu (available in Asian markets)
2 cups water
½ cup bonito flakes (available in Asian markets)

To make dashi: Place konbu and water in small pot over medium heat. When bubbles just begin to form around konbu, turn off heat. Remove konbu and set aside. Add bonito to water and let steep about 5 minutes. Strain.

Scrub kabocha well; cut in wedges and remove seeds. Do not peel. Place in 4- to 6-quart slow cooker.

Add mirin, soy sauce, and sugar to dashi broth. Stir to dissolve sugar, then pour over kabocha.

Cut reserved konbu into strips and sprinkle over kabocha. Cook 4 hours on low, until very soft.

Serve with cooking liquid.

{ BASIC ROAST KABOCHA } Brush wedges of kabocha with olive oil; sprinkle with salt and pepper. Pile into slow cooker and cook on low 3 to 4 hours, until tender but not too soft. Even a small kabocha makes a lot, which can be used many ways. Eat as is, or slice it for salads or to add to stir-fries or soups.

TIPS FOR CUTTING A KABOCHA

- Use the point of a knife to make a shallow cut into the kabocha near the bottom stem. Secure the widest part of the blade in the cut, press down, and rock back and forth until the kabocha splits.

- Use a paring knife to cut around the stem (this requires good wrist strength). Once you get a chunk out, switch to a bigger knife and cut wedges starting from the hole you just made.

- Position a cleaver just to the side of the stem and hit the cleaver with a mallet.

- Put the whole beast in the microwave on high about 3 minutes. The skin will then be soft enough to pierce.

Steamed Whole Artichokes with Sriracha Sauce

SERVES 8

*A*s a party dish, quartered artichokes offer a light alternative to the usual chip-and-dip appetizers. The segments make ideal finger food, each piece comprising a section of the heart and several leaves.

Four artichokes fit nicely in an oval pot at least 6 quarts in size. If you have a smaller round pot, you could make a single 'choke just for yourself.

4 large artichokes
12 garlic cloves
1 cup white wine (or water)
Juice of 1 lemon

Dip:

¼ cup mayonnaise
1 teaspoon Thai chili sauce (sriracha)

Cut off stems and tough outer leaves of each artichoke. Slice 1 inch off the top and cut off thorny leaf tips. Separate leaves slightly, rinse and drain well. Stand in slow cooker. Tuck garlic cloves among the leaves. Pour wine and lemon juice around artichokes. Cook on low 4 hours. To test for doneness, pull a leaf from the base of one artichoke; it should release easily.

To make dip: Combine mayonnaise and sriracha. Taste and add more chili sauce if desired.

When artichokes have cooled slightly, cut each one in quarters. Scoop out bristley choke and tiny inside leaves. The flesh will have a nice, lemony flavor.

Presentation is everything: Place dip in a bowl in center of round serving dish and arrange artichoke quarters around it like petals.

SLOW COOKING VEGETABLES

Think of your slow cooker as a miniature oven. Anything that takes about an hour to roast in an oven will do well in a slow cooker—whole root vegetables such as beets or potatoes, for example. Let them go on low for 4 to 6 hours (don't add any liquid), and they will essentially roast their way to tenderness.

Szechuan Eggplant with Daikon

SERVES 4

This is a classic stir-fry dish that cooks up nicely in a slow cooker. The daikon is not typical, but I find that it adds a little crunch to what is otherwise a rather mushy dish.

This recipe is scaled for a smaller cooker, but can be made in a larger one—you'll just need to check on it once in awhile, as the edges could cook faster and start to stick. The recipe is easily doubled and could be served as a vegetarian main dish.

1 pound long eggplant (about 3 medium), cut in 2-inch lengths on diagonal
1 small daikon, about 8 ounces, peeled, cut in 2-inch pieces, ½-inch thick

Sauce:

2 tablespoons soy sauce
2 tablespoons rice vinegar
1 tablespoon hoisin sauce
1 tablespoon chili-garlic sauce, or more to taste
1 tablespoon sesame oil
1 tablespoon grated ginger
3 cloves garlic, minced
1 tablespoon Minute tapioca

Pile eggplant and daikon in 4-quart slow cooker. Combine sauce ingredients and pour over vegetables, stirring so pieces are coated. Cook on high 3 to 4 hours or on low 6 hours, stirring occasionally for even cooking, until eggplant is very soft and daikon is tender. The tapioca will thicken the sauce.

Lemony Broccoli with Ginger Slivers

SERVES 6

This is a nice way to add a healthful side dish to dinner on leftover night, or when you're relying on takeout. It barely takes any time to prep, and can be put in the crock just before your evening starts to get crazy-busy, then allowed to cook as you tend to other things.

The broccoli emerges crisp-tender, as though lightly steamed, although its color will fade. The same technique could be used with cauliflower. Leftovers can be served cold mixed in with salads.

1 large bunch broccoli (about 1½ pounds), cut into spears
1 thumb-sized piece ginger, peeled and slivered
2 tablespoons lemon juice
¼ teaspoon salt

Place broccoli in 5- to 6-quart slow cooker. Sprinkle with ginger and lemon juice. Cook on low 90 minutes to 2 hours, until broccoli is crisp-tender. Served hot, broccoli will be very lemony. Tartness will mellow if chilled. Taste and sprinkle with salt just before serving. Serve with ginger slivers, which will soften and sweeten in the crock.

{ THINK SMALLER } A mini-crock can handle about ¾ pounds of broccoli—it may look too full, but the broccoli will cook down. This is a good amount for a small family.

Sweet Potatoes with Fruit and Mac Nuts

SERVES 8 OR MORE

T his recipe was one of my first favorites, from when I began trying to befriend my Crock-Pot in the early 2000s, using cookbooks mostly printed in the early '90s. It holds up well.

Consider this as a Thanksgiving side dish. It travels well and can be served at room temperature, making it ideal for potlucks.

1½ to 2 pounds sweet potatoes, peeled and diced
1 large Granny Smith apple, peeled, cored, diced
1 cup fresh cranberries
¾ cup firmly packed brown sugar
1 teaspoon ground cinnamon
¼ teaspoon ground nutmeg
2 tablespoons lemon juice
½ cup chopped macadamia nuts (or substitute pecans or almonds)

Combine sweet potatoes and apples in 5- or 6-quart slow cooker; sprinkle with cranberries.

Combine sugar, cinnamon, and nutmeg; sprinkle over top. Drizzle with lemon juice. Cook on low 6 to 8 hours, stirring occasionally, until potatoes are tender.

Toast nuts lightly in a dry skillet over medium heat. Sprinkle over cooked potatoes.

Mac-Nut Stuffing

SERVES 8

The slow cooker is a great way to make a ton of stuffing when you have no spare oven space. Use your favorite recipe, toasting the bread cubes for best results. A 6-quart crock will hold about 2 pounds of bread, or a standard loaf. Add sausage, onions, apples, celery, eggs, and any seasonings you like. Cook on low 4 to 6 hours. Stuffing will brown on top and will hold on the warm setting until dinner.

This stuffing has been a favorite of mine for many years. It's good enough for a holiday and simple enough for every-day use with, say, a roast chicken from the supermarket.

4 cups torn pieces of stale or toasted bread
1 cup crushed crackers
1 cup chopped macadamia nuts
1 large onion, chopped
½ cup EACH chopped basil and parsley
1 cup vegetable or chicken broth
2 eggs, beaten
½ teaspoon pepper
¼ cup butter, melted

Combine dry ingredients, onion, and herbs in 5-quart slow cooker. Combine broth, eggs, pepper, and butter; pour into pot. Toss. Cook on low 4 to 5 hours, stirring once, until puffy and brown around edges.

Spicy Bean and Corn Casserole

SERVES 6 TO 8

This casserole is an oh-so-easy side dish that emerges like a soft and light pudding studded with veggies. It could be varied with a few add-ins, such as canned chilies and/or shredded cheese. Leave out the minced chili peppers if you're serving a heat-averse crowd. Stir in some leftover shredded chicken, cubed bits of sausage or even Spam and you've got a one-dish meal.

3 cups fresh or thawed frozen corn
1 cup sliced long beans (½-inch slices)
1 to 2 small Hawaiian chili
    peppers, seeded and minced,
    or ½ teaspoon dried chili
    pepper
3 large eggs, beaten
½ teaspoon salt
1½ cups whole milk
1 tablespoon softened butter
2 tablespoons sugar
3 tablespoons cornstarch

Grease the interior of a 3-quart slow cooker with nonstick cooking spray. Combine all ingredients in prepared crock. Stir well. Cover and cook on low 4 hours, or until set in center.

{ NOTE } If your slow cooker is bigger than 3 quarts, find a baking dish that will fit inside your crock (perhaps a casserole dish or loaf pan). Place all the ingredients in that dish and put the dish inside the crock.

{ Enter the Entrée }

The best way to use a slow cooker to make work-aday life easier is to cook on the weekends and reheat on the weekdays. But I know, I know. What you want your slow cooker to do is make dinner while you're at work. This is the holy grail of slow cooking, and I'm sorry to say, not all recipes are conducive to cooking for nine or 10 hours.

That said, the holy grail is attainable. Some beef or pork dishes, especially those involving large cuts, can go for eight to 10 hours, and some bean dishes for 12. Check out the index by time on page 160 for some longer-cooking recipes.

Kare-Kare Oxtail Stew

SERVES 8 TO 10

K are-kare, or kari-kari, is a Filipino oxtail stew made with peanut butter. This version capitalizes on the slow cooker's ability to make an excellent stock, which serves as the basis for the stew's gravy.

Ground rice and achiote are traditionally used to thicken the stew and color it a pale orange, but if you'd rather simplify, use cornstarch or tapioca starch for thickening and live with the natural beige tone.

3 to 4 pounds oxtails
1 medium onion, sliced
2 cloves garlic, crushed
1 quart water
1 pound green beans, sliced into 2-inch lengths
3 small eggplant, sliced into 1-inch wedges
2 teaspoons achiote powder, sold in small packets near Filipino
    seasonings in Asian markets and some supermarkets
½ cup chunky peanut butter
½ cup toasted ground rice (see note)
1 teaspoon fish sauce

Place oxtails, onions, and garlic in 6- to 7-quart with water, adding a little more if needed just to cover oxtails. Cook on low 6 hours, or until meat is tender. Remove oxtails and onions. Strain stock and skim fat. Refrigerate oxtails and onions.

Return stock to pot; add beans, and eggplant. Cook on low 3 to 4 hours, until vegetables are tender. Stir in achiote powder, peanut butter, and ground rice, stirring to combine. Return oxtails and onions to pot. Continue cooking until oxtails are heated through and mixture is thickened. Drizzle with fish sauce.

{ VARIATIONS } Eggplant and beans are typically found in this dish, but other vegetables can be used, including greens such as bok choy, added at the end of the cooking time.

{ NOTE } To make ground rice, toast uncooked rice over medium heat in a dry skillet until golden. Grind in a coffee-grinder.

Short-Rib Stew
with Sweet Potatoes and Taro

SERVES 10

*U*ntil recently I hadn't met a slow cooker beef stew
that I could love. Turns out I was trusting in the
wrong recipes and the wrong cuts of beef.

Here's the correct answer: short ribs. After several
hours of cooking they emerge at just the right tenderness.
This recipe is based on one from Star-Advertiser reader
Joanne Naai. I strongly suggest you give it a try. It'll make
you all warm and happy inside.

3 pounds beef short ribs, about 1 inch thick (see note)
½ teaspoon salt
½ teaspoon pepper
1 large onion, halved and cut in wedges
3 stalks celery, minced
3 cloves garlic, minced
3 carrots, peeled and sliced in 1-inch lengths (about 1½ cups)
1 large Okinawan sweet potato, peeled and cut in chunks (about 3
   cups)
1 medium taro, peeled and cut in chunks (about 3 cups)
1 cup beef broth
1 (15-ounce) can tomato sauce
1 cup red wine
3 tablespoons tapioca starch
¼ cup water

Sprinkle ribs on both sides with salt and pepper. Cut into pieces between each bone.

Place onions in bottom of slow cooker. Top with celery and garlic,
then ribs, then carrots, sweet potato, and taro. Pour broth, tomato
sauce, and wine over top. Cook on low overnight, or at least 7 hours,
until meat is tender.

Transfer meat and vegetables to a bowl. Tilt slow cooker and skim fat. Dissolve tapioca starch in water. Stir into juices in pot and turn slow cooker to high for a few minutes to let juices thicken into a light gravy. (Or thicken gravy in a pot on the stovetop using tapioca starch dissolved in water.)

Taste and adjust seasonings with salt and pepper if necessary. Return meat (deboned if you like) and vegetables to slow cooker.

{ NOTE } You need thick-cut short ribs, not the thin type meant to make Korean kalbi. If you don't see any at the meat counter, press that buzzer and summon the butcher. Chances are you can order some up.

GO EASY ON THE LIQUID

Think of your slow cooker as a terrarium—not airtight, but closed in, so water does not evaporate. Just watch your cooker at work—no steam, right? There's no reduction, no condensing of flavors as there would be in a stewed, braised, or roasted dish prepared on the stove or in the oven. You can end up with too much liquid, and flavors that are insipid, not inspired. To overcome you must use water sparingly, in tandem with ingredients that boost flavor.

Isle-style roasts and stews do well in the slow cooker as long as you go easy on any liquid you use. Any ingredient, except dried beans, pasta, or rice, gives off water during cooking, so even if you start with just a cup you will open the pot to a lot of liquid. Two to four cups total liquid, including tomato sauce, soy sauce, or vinegar, is all you need, unless you're making a soup. Even if the meat is not covered in liquid, it will be by the time cooking ends. In fact, don't be afraid to put meat in the cooker dry—it will not burst into flames.

Chinese-Style Oxtail Stew

SERVES 6

This stew is rich with the flavors of anise and a Chinese rice wine called shaoxing. For vegetable notes it features shiitake mushrooms (splurge on fresh if possible) and white baby bok choy.

This dish is much improved if refrigerated overnight so the fat congeals and can be discarded. I got 5 ounces of fat out of my oxtails. On the second day, warm the gravy on the stove top, thicken it, then add the meat and greens and simmer until heated through.

Serve the oxtails in all their bony glory, or debone, if your dining audience prefers not to confront the reality of eating, well, tails.

5 pounds beef oxtails
1 cup Chinese rice wine (shaoxing, see note)
½ cup soy sauce
2 tablespoons brown sugar
3 star anise
2-inch piece ginger, cut in chunks and crushed
4 stalks lemongrass, tough green parts removed, crushed
3 large cloves garlic, crushed
1½ cups water
12 fresh shiitake mushrooms (or dried and reconstituted)
¼ cup tapioca starch or cornstarch dissolved in ¼ cup water
1 pound white baby bok choy (sometimes called pak choy or
    Shanghai cabbage) or other Chinese green such as choy sum

Parboil oxtails 10 to 15 minutes; discard water (this step can be skipped if your oxtails are not gristly or bloody).

Combine remaining ingredients, except tapioca starch and greens, in slow cooker. Add oxtails. Stir. Cook on low 8 hours, or until meat is very tender.

Remove oxtails and mushrooms from liquid. Strain liquid. Debone oxtails if desired. Refrigerate solids and liquid in separate containers overnight.

The next day, discard congealed fat from liquid (there will be a lot) and bring liquid to a simmer over medium heat. Taste and adjust seasonings by adding more soy sauce, sugar, or wine. Or, if flavor is too strong, add water. Gradually add tapioca starch mixture, stirring until liquid thickens to a light gravy (you may not need all the tapioca). Add oxtails, mushrooms, and bok choy. Simmer until heated through.

{ NOTE } Shaoxing, sometimes called yellow wine or "shao hsing," is a Chinese cooking wine made from fermented rice, found near other cooking wines or vinegars in Asian markets. To substitute use gin, dry sherry, or dry white wine.

Corned Beef
with Kim Chee and Guava
SERVES 10

*E*ven if your Crock-Pot makes few appearances in your life, March is the time to drag it out from under the counter behind the big pots. St. Patrick's Day corned beef is one of those foolproof slow-cooker meals: Put big slab o' meat in pot with liquid and spice packet, turn to low, go away for 10 hours.

Here is an alternative with local flavors. Idea credit goes to Wade Ueoka, a chef with Alan Wong's restaurant, who once made a corned beef soup using Italian sausage, russet potatoes, and savoy cabbage. This version uses kim chee and araimo, or Japanese taro, which cooks up buttery soft and absorbs all the flavors. A scoop of guava jelly provides a sweet edge and a rich, intriguing taste.

Warning: This dish is not at all lean. A variation at the end offers ways to cut the fat and sodium.

2½ to 3 pounds corned beef, cut in 10 to 12 chunks
1 large onion, in thin wedges
1 pound sausage (Italian, Portuguese or any other type)
4 large cloves garlic, crushed
1 to 2 teaspoons crushed red pepper
1 cup water
1 sprig rosemary
2 pounds araimo (small Japanese taro), peeled, or 2 large
    potatoes, peeled and cut in large pieces
12 ounces won bok or head cabbage kim chee, drained
½ cup guava jelly
4 cups spicy greens (watercress, sliced mustard cabbage, or other
    dark leafy greens)

Soak corned beef in water 1 hour; drain to reduce salt.

Place meat, onions, and sausage in 6-quart slow cooker. Add garlic.

Sprinkle with crushed pepper. Add water. Top with rosemary. Place araimo or potato on top (they will get too soft if mixed in with meat). Cook 8 to 9 hours on low.

Remove araimo or potatoes and rosemary. Stir in kim chee and jelly. Cook another hour, or until meat is tender.

Skim fat. Taste broth. If it is too salty, add 1 to 2 cups water. Mix in greens and let steep briefly until wilted. Return araimo or potatoes to pot.

{ TO REDUCE SODIUM AND FAT } Replace sausage with 2 cans garbanzo beans and/or eliminate kim chee and add another teaspoon chili peppers. You could also refrigerate the broth to let the fat solidify, then scoop it out.

Simpler Approaches

For basic Crock-Pot corned beef, place sliced onions in bottom of a 5- or 6-quart slow cooker. Lay a 3- to 4-pound corned beef on top, with contents of spice packet. Add 1 cup water or (better) beer. Place large pieces of carrots and potatoes on top. Cook on low 8 to 10 hours, until meat is very tender. Potatoes and carrots can be removed early if they are getting too soft. Add sliced cabbage to pot in last 30 minutes.

To add a little isle style, mix equal parts guava jelly and mustard and spread over corned beef before cooking. The broth will take on a deep, sweet flavor.

Corned beef also does well in the crock with no liquid. Soak it in water first, though, about 30 minutes to remove some of the salt. Rinse, drain, and put it in the crock with the contents of the spice packet and a coating of any fruit jelly. Surround the meat with some small potatoes and cook 8 to 10 hours. The texture of corned beef cooked this way is remarkable, tender but not as soft as it can get when cooked in water. The meat will give up lots of liquid while cooking, but it will be salty and should be discarded.

Hearty Poi Stew

P oi is a great way to thicken cooking liquids and create a creamy gravy. It's also a nutritional improvement over cornstarch, packing protein, fiber, and other good things—whereas cornstarch is just, well, starch.

2 pounds boneless beef short ribs, in 1-inch cubes
2 tablespoons soy sauce
2 teaspoons red pepper flakes
8 large cloves garlic, crushed and chopped
1 large onion, in wedges
2 cups potatoes, taro, or sweet potatoes in chunks
2 carrots, in 1-inch pieces, about 1½ cups
1 red bell pepper, diced
1 sprig rosemary
1 (14-ounce) can diced tomatoes (or 2 cups fresh)
1½ cups beef broth
½ cup red wine
1 cup poi

Place beef in a 6- or 7-quart slow cooker. Toss with soy sauce and pepper flakes. Add remaining ingredients except poi. Cook on low 6 to 8 hours, until meat is tender.

Skim fat from pot (tilting the crock makes this easier). Stir in poi and let cook 30 minutes longer, until gravy thickens.

{ OPTIONAL FIRST STEP } Beef can be browned before adding to pot, along with garlic and onions. This boosts the beef flavor and allows the aromatics to "bloom."

{ THINK GREEN } Add some color to the pot by stirring in some sliced kale, baby bok choy or 2-inch pieces of choy sum into the stew at the same time as the poi. Greens cook quickly and will keep their bright color when added at the end of cooking time.

{ VARIATION } Bone-in beef shanks also work well. Debone and slice the meat after cooking for easier eating.

SLOW

Chinese Chicken Curry Hot Pot

SERVES 6

Newspaper reader Melissa Pang Nikaido sent me the recipe for a family favorite, a chicken curry with bold flavors of ginger, curry, and oyster sauce. I have adapted it with a few ingredients you might find in a Chinese hot pot. Foo chuk (dried bean curd), dried shiitake mushrooms, cubes of fried tofu, and taro are easily found in Asian grocery stores, and the results are well worth the effort.

8 bone-in skinless chicken thighs
12 ounces taro, peeled and cubed
10 dried shiitake mushrooms, soaked in hot water to soften
4 sticks foo chuk (dried bean curd), soaked in hot water to soften
1 block (6 ounces) fried tofu, or aburage, soaked in hot water to remove excess oil, cut in squares
3 stalks green onion, for garnish

Seasonings:

1 tablespoon minced garlic
2-inch piece ginger, peeled and cut in slivers
2 to 3 tablespoons curry powder
1 tablespoon sugar
¼ cup sherry or red wine
1 cup chicken broth
¼ cup oyster sauce

Measure seasonings into crock and mix. Add chicken and taro; turn to coat pieces. Squeeze mushrooms, foo chuk, and tofu to remove excess water. Add to crock. Cook on low about 5 hours, until chicken and taro are tender. Stir halfway through if possible.

Top with green onion before serving.

{ TO REDUCE FAT } Remove chicken and other items from liquid in crock. Skim fat from liquid. (To make a thicker gravy, dissolve ¼ cup tapioca starch in ¼ cup water and stir into liquid; turn heat to high for a few minutes. This may also be done in a pot on the stove.) Return everything to the pot. (For ease of eating, chicken can be deboned first.)

Tips for slow cooking chicken:

- For best results, use bone-in chicken pieces, but remove the skin (this cuts oiliness). Thighs have the most flavor and are easy to slice for easy serving or for the most compact storage of leftovers. White meat tends to dry out.

- The biggest mistake people make when slow cooking chicken is overcooking. In most slow cookers, chicken will be done in just over four hours, although it can go longer for added tenderness. Don't let it cook too long, though, or the texture may turn dry and mealy.

Spicy Honey-Garlic Wings

SERVES 4 TO 6

Chicken wings are such tiny bits of meat, it's easy to infuse them with flavor. Cooking them in the slow cooker leaves them tender and tasty, but pale. A quick run under the broiler crisps the skin and gives them a delicious-looking tan.

4 pounds chicken wings
¼ cup sesame oil
2 tablespoons sesame seeds
2 tablespoons chopped green onion

Sauce:

¼ cup soy sauce
¼ cup mirin
¼ cup honey
2 tablespoons grated ginger, with juice
4 large cloves garlic, minced
1 teaspoon Thai chili sauce (Sriracha), or more to taste

Combine sauce ingredients in 6- or 7-quart slow cooker; stir well. Add chicken wings and toss to coat. Cook on low 4 hours, until cooked through.

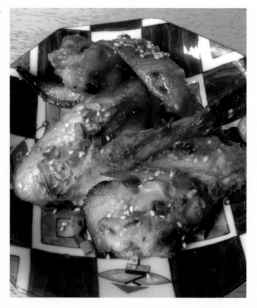

Arrange wings on rimmed cooking sheet. Brush with sesame oil and sprinkle with sesame seeds. Broil until nicely browned, 5 to 10 minutes. Sprinkle with green onions.

Spicy Miso Chicken

SERVES 6

T hanks to newspaper reader Keith Okazaki for sharing this recipe, a bright and flavorful approach to
chicken. Leftovers are great recycled in sandwich
wraps or served cold over a salad.

4 to 5 pounds bone-in chicken thighs (about 12 pieces), skin
   removed

Sauce:

1 cup beer, any kind
1 cup miso, any kind
1 cup brown sugar
2 cups chopped green onions
1-inch piece ginger, peeled and chopped
3 cloves garlic, chopped
1 tablespoon chili sauce, or to taste (sambal oelek or sriracha)

Combine sauce ingredients in 4- to 6-quart slow cooker, adding chili
sauce last, a teaspoon at a time, tasting as you go to reach desired
spiciness. Mix well. Add chicken, turning to coat. Cook on low 4 to 6
hours, until chicken is tender and cooked through.

{ NOTE } If you have time, this dish tastes better the next day.
Remove chicken from sauce, break meat into bite-size pieces
and discard bones. Refrigerate chicken and sauce separately.
The next day, skim fat from sauce and reheat, thickening with a
mixture of water and tapioca starch or cornstarch. Add chick-
en and heat through.

{ USING THE LEFTOVERS } Spicy Miso Chicken is ideal for turning into summer rolls. Moisten a rice paper wrap, spread shredded chicken in the center, add shredded lettuce and soba or
rice noodles. Fold in sides and roll up tightly. Serve with a dip
of chili sauce.

Korean-Style Chicken Thighs

SERVES 4

The flavors here are similar to Korean short ribs, or kalbi. Don't be concerned that the recipe calls for very little liquid. More will cook out of the chicken, creating a light sauce for serving. Double the recipe for a crowd, but be sure to turn the pieces during cooking or the ones on top will be very pale.

3 pounds bone-in skinless chicken thighs (5 to 6 pieces)
Sliced green onion, for garnish
Toasted sesame seeds, for garnish

Sauce:

2 tablespoons soy sauce
2 tablespoons sugar
1 tablespoon sesame oil
1 tablespoon chili-garlic sauce
1 tablespoon minced garlic

Place chicken in 5-quart slow cooker. Combine sauce ingredients and pour over chicken, turning pieces to coat. Cook on low 4 hours, until tender. Turn pieces once during cooking, if possible.

Remove chicken, debone, and slice. Skim fat from sauce, pour over chicken. Garnish with green onion and sesame seeds.

{ ADD SOME GREENS } Chinese greens, such as bok choy or choi sum, can be layered on top of the chicken to steam in the last hour of cooking. Just be aware that water will cook out of the greens and thin your sauce. For a thicker sauce, simmer it on the stovetop with a cornstarch slurry. Serve the greens mixed in with the chicken slices.

Stuffed Pork Chop Pasteles

S tar-Advertiser *reader Rose Soto learned to make pasteles the traditional Puerto Rican way from her mother. It's a labor-intensive task that begins with grinding green bananas and involves steaming, sautéing, simmering, layering, wrapping, and steaming again.*

She developed this version for a slow cooker using thick pork chops that she stuffs, then piles into the pot with a hearty tomato sauce. The bananas are still ground and steamed in packets to make a firm masa that is sliced and added to the slow cooker.

Pasteles can be made into a two-day project, with the banana masa made one day, the pork chops the next. For those who believe the masa is the best part of the pasteles, that portion of the recipe can be doubled. There will be enough room in the pot.

7 to 8 thick pork chops (see note)
¼ cup cider vinegar
1 tablespoon vegetable oil
1 teaspoon seasoned salt
1 cup EACH chopped cilantro, onions, and bell peppers (red, green, or a mix)
2 cups chopped green onion (1 bunch)
3 cloves garlic, crushed
1 cup hot chicken broth
1 (6-ounce) can pitted whole black olives, drained
1 (6-ounce) can tomato paste
1 cup hot water
½ teaspoon EACH oregano, cumin, and curry powder

Masa:

4 green bananas
1 small potato
1 teaspoon EACH garlic salt, white pepper, onion powder, and cayenne flakes
½ cup achiote oil (see note)

continued on the next page

Stuffing:

1 (6-ounce) box chicken-flavor stove-top stuffing mix
1½ cups chicken broth
¾ cup prepared masa

To make masa: Peel bananas and cut into thirds. Place in bowl of cold water to keep from turning brown. Peel potato and cut in wedges, put in water with bananas. Grind banana and potato in juicer or food processor to make a paste. Season with salt and spices. Stir in achiote oil.

Bring a pot of water to boil. Set aside ¾ cup masa for the stuffing. Wrap remaining masa in foil packets (place about ½ cup on greased sheet of foil and fold foil around masa to make packet). You should have 3 to 4 packets. Drop into boiling water, then let simmer 45 minutes.

Remove from water and chill. (Packets could also be cooked in the slow cooker: Pour 2 to 3 cups boiling water into cooker, add packets, and cook on high about 3 hours, until firm).

Rinse pork chops, let drain in colander, then pat dry. Drizzle with vinegar and let sit 20 minutes.

Meanwhile, make stuffing according to directions on box, using chicken broth in place of water. Remove from heat and stir in reserved masa.

Cut a slit deep into each pork chop, cutting to make a pocket for the stuffing (a thin serrated knife such as a steak knife works well). Fill chops with stuffing and secure the open edge with toothpicks or bamboo skewers.

Heat oil in large skillet. Brown chops well on both sides, sprinkling with seasoned salt.

Place cilantro, onion, bell peppers, green onion, and garlic in bottom of 7-quart slow cooker. Top with chicken broth. Stand browned chops in cooker with cut edge up. Top with olives.

Mix tomato paste in hot water and stir until smooth. Add oregano, cumin, and curry powder. Pour mixture over chops. Cook on low 6 to 8 hours, until chops are cooked through. Once mixture in slow cooker is simmering (about 4 to 5 hours), remove masa from foil packets and cut in ½-inch slices. Add to slow cooker. Finish cooking.

{ SELECTING CHOPS } Soto prefers bone-in pork chops 1½ to 2 inches thick. Boneless chops, however, are more uniform and easier to stuff. Also, it is easier to cut a slit for the stuffing if the chops are partially frozen.

{ TO MAKE ACHIOTE OIL } Stir 1 teaspoon achiote powder into ½ cup hot water and 2 tablespoons vegetable oil. Stir to dissolve powder. Soto uses the Sa-son brand of powdered achiote, which includes ground coriander, available in some Asian markets. Plain achiote powder can be found in small packages in Asian markets and near the Filipino seasonings in many supermarkets. The powder is added mostly for coloring, so the plain is an adequate substitute.

Hoisin-Guava Baby Back Ribs

SERVES 6

Ribs are perfect for the slow cooker. Made tender and flavorful through long, slow cooking, they're usually prepared in an oven, on a grill, or in a smoker. It can be high-maintenance. A Crock-Pot version will take hours, but you don't even have to be in the building.

You could do without the broiling and glazing at the end—but if you take the trouble you will be so much happier.

5 to 6 pounds pork baby back ribs
Pepper, to taste
2 tablespoons cornstarch dissolved in ¼ cup water

Sauce:

1 (8.5 ounce) jar hoisin sauce, about 1 cup
1 (10-ounce) jar guava jelly
¼ cup red wine, dry sherry or whisky
2-inch piece ginger, peeled, smashed, and minced, about ¼ cup
6 cloves garlic, minced
2 teaspoons red pepper flakes

Season ribs with pepper and stand upright around sides of a 6-quart slow cooker. Meaty sides should face outward, with the thicker part of the ribs at the bottom. Overlap slabs if necessary.

Combine sauce ingredients, pour over ribs. Cook on low until tender, 6 to 8 hours. Ribs should not be so soft that the meat is falling off the bone.

Place ribs on a greased broiling rack, meaty side down. Preheat broiler.

Skim fat from liquid in slow cooker; strain 2 cups into saucepan over medium heat. Stir in cornstarch slurry, and simmer until thickened.

Brush ribs with thickened sauce and broil until beginning to brown, 2 to 4 minutes. Turn ribs, brush with more sauce and broil until well browned and sticky, about 10 minutes longer. Brush with more sauce occasionally.

Let rest 5 minutes. Slice ribs; serve with extra sauce.

{ EASY DOES IT } The simplest approach to slow cooker ribs relies on store-bought barbecue sauce. I like the Spicy Hawaiian Bar-B-Q Sauce from Noh Foods. Stand ribs around the crock, squeeze the juice from 1 lemon over ribs, followed by most of a bottle of sauce (save some). Once cooked, ribs can be broiled and glazed with extra sauce. Or serve them straight from the crock, with sauce for dipping.

Sweet-Sour Pig's Feet

SERVES 6

This tangy, hearty dish is often served to new mothers as a way of restoring strength in the days after childbirth. Others crave it for its simple, puckery chewiness. Be sure to serve the slices of ginger with the meat—they will be tender, mellow, and a delicious complement.

3 pounds pig's feet
1 pound ginger, in thin slices
1 pound wong tong (see notes), broken in pieces
1 cup black vinegar (see notes)
½ cup white or cider vinegar

Bring large pot of water to boil and parboil pig's feet about 10 minutes, then rinse and drain to remove impurities. Place in 6- or 7-quart slow cooker. Arrange ginger and wong tong pieces around pig's feet. Pour vinegar over all. Cook on low about 8 hours. Taste juices and add more vinegar if desired. Remove everything from pot except liquid. Skim fat from juices. Spoon juices over meat.

{ OPTIONAL ADDITIONS } 1 cup raw peanuts, shelled; 6 hard-cooked eggs, peeled; 8 to 10 whole dried shiitake mushrooms, soaked and squeezed dry; 1 large bunch dark Chinese greens (such as bok choy or mustard cabbage), in 2-inch segments. Peanuts should be stirred in at the beginning of cooking, eggs and mushrooms in the last 1 to 2 hours, greens at the very end (lay on top and let steam).

{ IF MAKING AHEAD } Refrigerate meat separately from juices. Before heating, remove fat from top of juices and bring juices to simmer in saucepan over medium heat, thickening if desired with a mixture of cornstarch or tapioca starch and water. Place meat and ginger slices in sauce to warm.

{ VARIATION } My mother makes this with fresh ham shanks instead of feet. The pieces tend to be more uniform in size.

{ INGREDIENT NOTES } Wong tong (slabs of Chinese brown sugar) and black vinegar (an inky vinegar derived from rice) can be found in Chinatown markets, Asian markets, and some supermarkets.

Deconstructed Laulau
SERVES 8

Laulau is lovely, but it ain't easy. Wrapping and tying those little bundles, then watching over a steaming pot for several hours ... it's just not a project for the lazy. This layered laulau does away with all that while maintaining the lū'au flavor. Your guests won't get a personal wrapped bundle—instead they'll get a generous scoop of laulau. They won't mind.

2 pounds lū'au leaves, trimmed of stems and fibrous parts
3 pounds pork butt, cut in large chunks, fat trimmed
3 teaspoons liquid smoke, divided
¼ cup sea salt, divided
Ti leaves to line crock
1 pound sweet potato, scrubbed, cut in ¾-inch slices
2 pounds chicken thighs, bone-in, skin and excess fat removed

Blanch lū'au leaves in pot of boiling water, cooking 2 to 3 minutes until wilted (otherwise leaves will not fit in pot). Rub pork with 2 teaspoons liquid smoke and 2 tablespoons salt.

Line bottom of 6-quart slow cooker with ti leaves. Top with pork pieces. Cover with half the lū'au leaves. Sprinkle with 1 tablespoon salt. Top with sweet potato and remaining lū'au leaves. Cover with more ti leaves. Cook on low 2 hours.

Rub chicken thighs with remaining liquid smoke and salt. Lift ti leaves and nestle chicken into lū'au leaves so they are mostly covered. Replace ti leaves. Cook 4 to 5 more hours, until chicken is falling off bone and pork is very tender.

Discard ti leaves. Remove chicken bones and tear chicken into bite-size pieces (it will pull apart easily). Serve out of crock or spoon into deep serving dish, arranging pork, chicken, lū'au leaves, and sweet potato in separate layers. Pour juices from pot over all.

SLOW

{ NOTE } If desired, 2 large pieces of salted butterfish may be tucked just under the top layer of ti leaves in the last hour of cooking. Put a ti leaf under the fish as well, to keep the bones out of the pot.

{ TRADITIONAL LAULAU } Foil-wrapped bundles of laulau can be steamed in a slow cooker, but even a 7- or 8-quart cooker won't hold many. Make small bundles so you can better fit them into the crock. You'll need a rack in the bottom, or fashion one out of coils of foil—you just need to keep the laulau from touching the water. Pour boiling water into the pot about an inch deep, then place bundles on rack. Cook 7 hours on low. Add more water if needed as laulau cooks. (Tip: Wrap one bundle so it easy to open to check whether the meat is cooked.)

Green Tea-Flavored Kālua Pork

SERVES 8

Kālua pork is one of those fail-safe beginner dishes for the slow cooker. Rub a pork roast with sea salt and cook away. After eight hours or so it will be fall-apart tender with a pot full of juices.

This recipe kicks up the concept with the intriguing addition of tea leaves, based on a Korean technique used with pork belly. The idea is to replace the smoke of the imu with the slight smokiness of tea leaves. Of course, you could also use liquid smoke, but tea is more subtle and gives the pork a sweetness that will leave people wondering exactly what you did to get this flavor.

3 pound boneless pork butt
3 tablespoons green tea leaves (about 6 tea bags worth)
2 tablespoons sea salt
Ti leaves to line slow cooker

Pat pork butt dry. Combine tea leaves and salt. Rub all over pork. Wrap in plastic wrap and refrigerate overnight.

Line bottom and sides of slow cooker with ti leaves. Unwrap pork and place in slow cooker. Top with another piece of ti leaf. Do not add water. Cook on low 8 to 10 hours, until very tender.

Remove pork to cutting board and let rest 5 minutes. Skim fat from juices. Shred pork. (The tea leaves will look like pepper flakes; you can scrape some off if they bother you, but those that remain will not be a distraction in taste or texture.) Use some juices to moisten pork, but go easy as the juices will be salty.

SLOW ONO LŪʻAU

An imu provides hours of long, slow cooking—steaming and tenderizing foods. A slow cooker does much the same, without the hole in the ground and the fire. All told—much more practical, especially for those who don't have much of a backyard. Or a shovel.

Beyond that, traditional Hawaiian dishes are among the easiest and most foolproof in the slow-cooker repertoire. Many are simple enough to require no formal recipes. Some easy examples:

- { BASIC KĀLUA PORK } Rub 3- to 5-pound pork butt with a few drops liquid smoke (not too much, it's strong), then rub with salt. Place in a slow cooker lined with ti leaves and cook 6 to 8 hours on low, until easily shredded. Moisten shredded pork with defatted juices from pot.

- { KĀLUA ALTERNATIVES } The same kālua process can also be used for chicken (whole or pieces) or turkey (breast or legs). Cooking time will be about 4 hours for chicken; 6 hours for turkey. Chef Alan Wong told me he once slow-cooker kālua-ed a 5-pound ham, minus the salt.

- { KĀLUA PORK AND CABBAGE } Make Kālua Pork, but add 4 to 6 cups shredded cabbage to liquid in pot; let steep with heat off until wilted. Stir in shredded pork.

- { LŪʻAU STEW } Rub chunks of beef stew meat (about 3 pounds) with sea salt and a little liquid smoke. Layer in pot with lūʻau leaves (if using a lot of leaves, blanch them first in boiling water so they'll fit in the crock). If you want it soupy, add 1 cup water. Cooking time will be 6 to 8 hours.

- { CHICKEN LŪʻAU } Like Lūʻau Stew, but use 4 to 6 skinless chicken thighs and 1 cup water; cook 4 hours. Shred or cut up meat after it's cooked and stir 1 cup coconut milk into pot. It is better to precook the leaves to be sure to eliminate that itchy feeling that undercooked lūʻau leaves can leave in the mouth and throat.

- { ROASTED SWEET POTATOES OR TARO } Scrub whole potatoes or taro and rub with vegetable oil and sea salt. Roast in slow cooker 8 to 10 hours, until easily pierced with a fork. Slice and serve.

Isle-Style Pulled Pork Sandwiches

SERVES 8

This recipe is a contribution from my friend Hayley Matson-Mathes, who calls it her version of kālua pork, although the seasonings she's added give it a different flavor from the lūʻau standard.

I've adapted it to make pulled-pork sandwiches on taro buns. It would also be great with steamed buns, the type served with Peking duck in Chinese restaurants. Add a dab of hoisin sauce and some green onion slivers. Yum.

4 to 5 pounds boneless pork shoulder or butt
2 tablespoons olive oil
1 large onion, sliced
16 taro buns

Sauce:

½ cup soy sauce
¼ cup brown sugar
2 teaspoons sea salt
1 teaspoon pepper
2 teaspoons grated ginger
2 teaspoons liquid smoke
1 teaspoon minced garlic
½ teaspoon Chinese five spice

Place pork in 6- or 7-quart slow cooker. Combine sauce ingredients and pour over pork. Cook on low 6 to 8 hours, or until pork shreds easily with a fork. Remove meat to cutting board and shred. Heat oil in skillet. Brown onions over medium heat.

Strain juices and skim fat. Pour over meat.

Slice buns in half and toast lightly. Fill with shredded meat and grilled onions. May be served with barbecue sauce.

Portuguese Sausage, Beans, and Beer

SERVES 10

*A*ny type of sausage can be used here, from kielbasa to Lit'l Smokies. Add some crusty bread and you have a complete meal. The flavor is brightened after cooking by stirring in something acidic. I like vinegar, but you could try lime juice if you prefer.

1 pound dried black-eyed peas or other small bean, picked over and rinsed
1 (10-ounce) Portuguese sausage, in half-inch slices
1 (12-ounce) bottle beer, at room temperature (see note)
2 cups water
1 (14-ounce) can diced tomatoes
6 large cloves garlic, crushed
1 sprig rosemary
1 onion, minced
¼ cup brown sugar
1 teaspoon red chili flakes
1 tablespoon balsamic vinegar or lime juice
4 cups spinach leaves or sliced kale

Combine all ingredients except vinegar or lime juice and kale in 6- or 7-quart slow cooker. Cook on low 9 to 11 hours, until beans are tender. Remove rosemary sprig. Stir in vinegar or lime juice. Add some hot water if beans are too thick. Turn off heat and stir in spinach or kale.

{ ABOUT THE BEER } Use a light-colored beer such as a lager. Dark beers may turn bitter.

{ IF YOU HAVE TIME } Diced carrots and potatoes can be added at the beginning of cooking. Other vegetables, such as bell peppers, can be added halfway through cooking time.

Lasagna, Like Magic

SERVES 8

This was the recipe that restored my faith in my slow cooker. Like magic it takes sauce, spices, and uncooked pasta noodles and turns them into lasagna. First time I tried it, everything went into the pot and we went to the movies. Came home to a hot, chewy, gooey dinner.

Aha, said I, this is what a slow cooker is supposed to do. Make life easier. So even though lasagna isn't really local-style food, I include this recipe because it marked the beginning of my journey.

½ pound ground turkey
½ pound (2 links) hot Italian sausage
1 cup chopped onion
2 cloves garlic, minced
1 (29-ounce) can tomato sauce
1 (6-ounce) can tomato paste
1 tablespoon fresh or 1 teaspoon dried oregano
1 tablespoon fresh or 1 teaspoon dried rosemary
1 pound nonfat cottage cheese
1 pound shredded mozzarella cheese
1 (13-ounce) box whole-wheat lasagna noodles, uncooked
1 small zucchini, thinly sliced
1 (10-ounce) package frozen chopped spinach, thawed and
  squeezed of all liquid
½ cup grated Parmesan cheese

Lightly brown ground turkey, sausage, onion, and garlic (don't cook until well done or it will toughen in slow cooker). Add tomato sauce, tomato paste, oregano, and rosemary. Stir well, heating just long enough to warm sauce.

Combine cottage cheese and mozzarella.

Grease inside of a 6- or 7-quart slow cooker (see note). Spoon about 1 cup meat sauce onto bottom of slow cooker, covering well. Top with layer of uncooked noodles (break to fit, using small pieces to fill gaps). Top noodles with half of cheese mixture. Add more sauce, another layer of noodles and remaining cheese. Layer spinach and zucchini over top layer of cheese. Top with final layer of noodles. Pour remaining sauce over top. Sprinkle with Parmesan cheese. Cover and cook on low 4 hours or until noodles are tender. Turn off pot and remove cover for a few minutes to let noodles set.

{ NOTE } This recipe is designed for an oval slow cooker. If yours is round you probably will have more than 3 layers of noodles.

Liliko'i BBQ Beans
SERVES 8

These beans take their sweetness from liliko'i jelly, which can be subbed with guava or the fruit flavor of your choice. It also uses brewed coffee for balance, a tip I learned from Slow Cooker Revolution by the editors of Cook's Illustrated.

This is a vegetarian dish, but you could easily stir in sausage or diced ham and let it heat through for about 10 minutes.

1 pound dry pinto beans
1 cup liliko'i (passion fruit) jelly
½ cup barbecue sauce
½ cup brewed coffee
1½ cups chopped onion
4 cloves garlic, minced
1 cup chopped red bell pepper (in large chunks)
¼ cup chopped cilantro
1 tablespoon minced fresh rosemary (or 1 teaspoon dried)
4 cups water

Combine ingredients in slow cooker. Cook on low 9 to 11 hours, until beans are tender.

Taste and adjust seasonings. Stir in more jelly or barbecue sauce, or add mustard, chili pepper sauce, or brown sugar as needed. Let sit about 10 minutes or hold on warm setting for up to an hour to allow to thicken slightly (add hot water if mixture becomes too thick).

{ NOTES } To shorten cooking time, beans may be cooked on high setting in 5 to 7 hours, or soak overnight in cold water before cooking.

SLOW COOKER BEAN BASICS

Why bother with dry beans when opening a can is so easy? Well, because with canned beans you get extra sodium, preservatives, and other such nasty things. With dry beans you get … beans. High in fiber and good for you.

Using a slow cooker makes it effortless. Dump beans and water in the cooker (for a pound of beans, 6 to 8 cups of water should be sufficient), let it go on low 8 to 12 hours, depending on the size of the beans. When they're tender, they're done.

Divide the beans into 2-cup servings—about the amount that comes in a can—and refrigerate or freeze. To conserve space, use Ziploc bags. Use as needed in soups, salads and stews.

One caveat: Beware kidney beans. I've been slow-cooking them for years without incident, but food safety experts now warn that these beans contain high levels of a toxin called Phytohaemagglutinin that can cause nausea and stomach distress. The toxin is killed when beans are cooked at high heat, but a slow cooker doesn't always reach the necessary temperature. In fact, cooking at low heat may actually increase toxicity. Dry kidney beans should be pre-cooked in boiling water for 10 minutes before adding them to a slow cooker. Some other beans also carry this toxin in smaller amounts. If you have a sensitive stomach, precooking is best with all beans, to be safe.

Pre-cooking—or at least pre-soaking—cuts cooking time for any type of bean. Soak dry beans overnight in cold water, then rinse and drain. Add to the slow cooker with fresh water and cooking time will be 6 to 8 hours on low. Crank it up to high if they're just not cooking fast enough (or if you're getting impatient). Ten minutes of boiling first will cut cooking time a bit more, but does mean getting out another pot, so the choice is up to you.

For extra flavor, use a portion of flavorful liquid (beer, red wine, chicken broth), ¼ or ½ cup of something sweet (sugar, brown sugar, honey, jelly of any type), some herbs (a sprig of rosemary is great, or roughly chopped basil, parsley, or oregano), or the aromatics of your choice (onions, garlic, ginger, or a combination). Stir in something acidic (vinegar, lemon juice), to brighten the taste at the end. Something salty may also be necessary (doesn't have to be salt, it can be soy sauce or fish sauce).

Paniolo Chili

SERVES 12

This is a slow-cooker version of my go-to chili recipe, which is in turn based on the first-place winner of the 1999 Great Hawaiian Chili Cookoff, by Jerry Hall of Ewa Beach. On the chili competition circuit, beans are frowned upon, but in my family it ain't chili without those beans, so my recipe includes them, without apology.

1½ pounds boneless cross-rib roast, cut in ½-inch cubes
1 pound boneless pork butt, cut in ½-inch cubes
6 cloves garlic, crushed
1 large onion, diced
½ pound Portuguese sausage
1 large red bell pepper, diced
1 large green bell pepper, diced
2 cans kidney beans, with liquid
½ cup chili powder
¼ cup cumin
2 cups chicken broth (or 1 15-ounce can)
1 (15-ounce) can tomato sauce
1 small red chile pepper, minced, or 1 teaspoon red pepper flakes

If desired, brown meat, garlic and onions lightly in a skillet with 2 tablespoons vegetable oil. If you'd rather not bother, just combine all the ingredients in a 6- or 7-quart slow cooker. Stir. Cook on low 4 to 6 hours, until meat is tender. Taste and adjust for spiciness.

{ NOTE } If you prefer using dry beans, soak them in water for as long as 24 hours before cooking. Use pinto beans instead of kidneys.

Thai-Style Vegetable Curry with Chickpeas
SERVES 8

f you are intimidated by the long list of ingredients, just pick your one favorite vegetable and use 5 cups of it in place of the variety called for here. This mix, though, provides a melange of tastes and textures, tied together with a bright, spicy Thai curry sauce.

2 cups canned chickpeas (garbanzo beans, see note)
2 cups diced potatoes (red or russet)
2 small eggplant, cut into 1-inch pieces
2 cups cauliflower florets
1½ cups long beans, cut in 2-inch pieces
1 cup chopped carrots
1 large onion, chopped
4 cups chicken or vegetable broth
6 cloves garlic, minced
2 tablespoons grated ginger, with juice
1 stalk lemongrass, tough outer layers removed, minced
¼ cup chopped cilantro
2 cups cherry tomato halves
1 (13-ounce) can coconut milk
2 tablespoons lime juice
1 tablespoon fish sauce
1 to 2 tablespoons Thai red or green curry paste (available in Asian section of supermarkets)

Combine ingredients through the cilantro in 6- or 7-quart slow cooker. Cook on low 6 hours until potatoes and carrots are tender. Stir in remaining ingredients. Taste and add more curry paste if needed. Let cook another 30 minutes.

〔 NOTE 〕 If you prefer using dry beans, soak them in water for as long as 24 hours before cooking.

With extra effort:

- If you find that in your slow cooked carrot dishes emerge under-cooked or onions are harsh in flavor, you can precook them in the microwave, on high in 3 tablespoons vegetable oil. Adding the garlic, too, helps the flavors of the aromatics "bloom."

- To keep eggplant from becoming too soft, wait until the 3-hour mark to add it to the pot.

- This dish creates a thin sauce. To thicken, add 2 tablespoons Minute tapioca at the beginning of the cooking time.

Spanish Rice

SERVES 10

Spanish Rice doesn't sound local, but we all ate in in our school cafeterias so it is by adoption an island food. This recipe feeds a crowd and is easier than making such a large amount on the stovetop because you don't have to worry about scorching.

Rice cooks up softer in a slow cooker, as it is steamed more than boiled. As a result, the texture of this dish won't be the same as the version your cafeteria lady made.

Note that it is important to start with hot broth. This not only speeds up the cooking time but keep the rice from getting mushy.

3 cups chicken broth or stock
1 pound ground turkey
1 onion, chopped (about 1 cup)
4 large cloves garlic, minced
1½ cups raw rice (white, brown
    or a mix)
28 ounces canned diced
    tomatoes
3 tablespoons tomato paste
2 tablespoons chili powder
1 tablespoon minced fresh
    rosemary
5 to 6 ounces Portuguese
    sausage, in ½-inch pieces
1 large green bell pepper, chopped

Bring chicken broth to a boil. Meanwhile, sauté ground turkey with onion and garlic until meat is lightly browned. Don't cook it too well done; it will finish cooking in the slow cooker. Scoop into 6- or 7-quart slow cooker.

Add remaining ingredients and stir well. Pour hot broth over all. Cook on high 2 to 3 hours, adding more water if mixture seems too thick. Brown rice may take longer.

Collard Greens with Smoked Turkey

SERVES 4

*C*ollards are extremely nutritious dark, leafy greens that are becoming increasingly available from local farms. They're often cooked until very tender—similar to lūʻau leaves—but they can also be enjoyed lightly cooked, while they've still got some bite. They pair well with smoked meats and are very good companions for the slow cooker, as the long cooking time leaves them infused with tons of flavor. This dish uses smoked turkey, easy to find in most supermarkets, but you could substitute a ham shank.

1 to 2 pounds collard greens
¼ to ½ cup vegetable oil
¼ cup minced garlic
1 large onion, diced
1 cup hot chicken or turkey stock
1 pound smoked turkey pieces
  (neck, wing or whatever you
  can find)

Strip stems from collard greens, then roughly chop leaves.

Heat oil in skillet over medium-high; add garlic and onions, stirring until onions are softened. Add to crock with collards and stock; stir. The hot stock will wilt the greens slightly and help them fit in the crock. Place turkey pieces on top. Cook on low 6 to 8 hours, until greens are tender. Turkey will be fall-apart tender.

Remove turkey pieces, let cool slightly, then debone. Combine collards and turkey meat in serving dish.

Shoyu Turkey Breast

SERVES 2 TO 4

Those who love turkey probably don't eat it as often as they'd like just because the birds are so darn big and roasting them is such a project. Here's a solution: a turkey breast slow-cooked to tender doneness. This lets you enjoy turkey year-round, or it's useful at Thanksgiving if you're feeding a smaller group and don't want to deal with a whole bird.

I owe Phyllis Good's Stock the Crock (Oxmoor House, $21.99) for the basic technique and the herb blend that gives the white meat a nice browned exterior, not the usual pale tinge of Crock-Pot poultry.

½ cup turkey, chicken or beef broth
¼ cup white wine
1½ teaspoons soy sauce
½ teaspoon pepper
½ teaspoon paprika
½ teaspoon EACH dried mustard, ground turmeric and dried
    tarragon
3-pound boneless turkey breast, thawed if frozen (see note)

Grease the interior of a 7-quart oval slow cooker with nonstick cooking spray. Place all ingredients except turkey into crock; stir. Settle turkey breast into liquid, then turn it, or use a spoon to make sure all sides are coated. Cover; cook on high 1 hour.

Reduce heat to low and continue cooking about 3 hours, or to an internal temperature of 160°F.

Remove turkey to a platter and tent with foil. Let sit a few minutes before carving.

The liquid left in the crock may be saved for stock or used to make gravy.

{ NOTE } If you can find a bone-in turkey breast it will also work in this recipe, but it is likely to be larger so double the other ingredients. Frozen boneless breasts (Jennie-O brand) are available in local markets.

Dashi-Based Cioppino

SERVES 6 TO 8

For this flavorful fish stew you'll need to search out shrimp with heads still attached. For this, Asian markets are a better bet than chain supermarkets. The shrimp heads and shells go into the broth, combined with konbu and bonito flakes, the basis of the traditional Japanese soup stock called dashi. The shrimp itself goes into the stew.

You can customize this with your choice of seafood: scallops or squid, for example. Squid will take longer to cook, though, so add it to the pot with the tomatoes and wine.

¼ small kabocha squash, thinly sliced, optional
1 cup chopped tomatoes
1 cup dry white wine (pinot grigio or sauvignon blanc are good choices and the rest of the bottle will make a good pairing with the finished dish)
1 pound firm white fish (such as swordfish, mahimahi or ahi), in 1-inch cubes
1 pound shrimp, peeled
1 pound Manilla clams

Dashi broth:

4 cups water
Heads and shells from 1 pound shrimp
2 tablespoons EACH minced garlic, shallot, and cilantro stems
4-inch square piece konbu (dried kelp)
2 cups bonito flakes

Combine stock ingredients except bonito flakes in a 6- to 7-quart slow cooker. Cook on high 2 hours. Turn off heat, add bonito flakes and let steep 10 minutes. Strain broth and return to pot.

Add kabocha, if using, tomatoes and wine. Return heat to high and let cook until kabocha is tender, about 1 hour. (If you need to slow things down so you can go out and run an errand, cook on low for 2 to 3 hours.)

Stir in seafood and let cook 30 minutes, until fish is cooked through and clams have opened.

{ TIP } If possible, take seafood out of refrigerator 20 minutes before adding to soup, to take the chill off. This keeps the temperature of the broth from dropping too much when the seafood is added.

{ VARIATIONS } In place of the kabocha, add color to the pot with other vegetables such as zucchini, halved cherry tomatoes or snow peas. Peas should be added with the seafood so they cook lightly.

{ LEFTOVERS } If you find the seafood is eaten but you still have lots of broth left, save it and reheat it with fresh seafood within the week. The first round of seafood will have added a new layer of flavor to the liquid.

Ginger-Lime Salmon Fillets

SERVES 2

We tend to think of our slow cookers only in terms of hours of unattended cooking. But there are other ways this device can make a busy life an easier one. Let's say you have to take the kids to soccer practice at 4 p.m., or you want to go to a yoga class at 5, or you have to walk the dog precisely at 6.

A dish like this one with a shorter cooking time can be started just before you leave and be ready for serving when you get back, so that on these busy evenings you don't have to rely on takeout or rush around trying to assemble a meal in 20 minutes.

Gentle low heat produces a delicate, soft fillet, and the vibrant flavors in the sauce brighten the taste. This dish is simple, yet scores a high impact. I used salmon because it is easy to find year-round, but any firm-fleshed fish would work. If you luck into some nice swordfish or mahimahi from local waters, give it a try.

2 (8- to 10-ounce) salmon fillets
2 ti leaves, trimmed to fit slow cooker insert
Chopped green onion, slivered ginger and thin lime slices, for
  garnish

Marinade:

1 tablespoon grated ginger with juice
1 tablespoon fresh lime juice
2 tablespoons soy sauce
2 tablespoons sugar

Combine marinade ingredients, stirring to dissolve sugar, and pour over fish. Let marinate 30 minutes.

Remove fillets, and place on top of ti leaf in 5- to 7-quart slow cooker. Cover with second ti leaf. Pour marinade over fish. Cook on low

60 to 90 minutes, until salmon is cooked through (it should flake easily with a fork). Remove to serving dish. Spoon sauce from cooker over fish. Garnish as desired.

{ HIGHER YIELD } This recipe is easily doubled, as long as the fillets will fit in your slow cooker in a single layer. Cutting fillets in smaller pieces can allow you to fit in more.

Chinese-Style Steamed Fish

SERVES 2

*S*low cooking is often large-scale cooking. The size of a crock lets you cook for a crowd. A steamed fish is a more intimate affair, its size held to the length of your oval crock (can't do this in a round crock, sorry). A 2-pound fish is about the limit, and the tail fin may still be sticking out. The slow cooker makes this type of preparation possible for those who don't have the right sized pot to steam a whole fish on the stove.

1 (2-pound) whole mullet, kumu, or Thai snapper, cleaned
2 cups boiling water
Chopped cilantro, for garnish

Marinade:

1 piece chung choi (salted turnip, available in Asian markets)
2 tablespoons soy sauce
2 tablespoons red wine
2 teaspoons cornstarch
2 teaspoons vegetable oil
2 stalks green onion, minced
2-inch piece ginger, minced

To prepare crock: Place a rack or coil of foil in bottom of a 6- to 7-quart slow cooker. Top with an oval plate long enough to hold the fish. Put a ti leaf on plate or form a doubled piece of foil into a shape that will hold the fish. Pour boiling water into crock and turn it on high. Let heat 30 minutes, until steamy.

Meanwhile, prepare fish: Chop chung choi, soak in water 5 minutes, squeeze dry. Combine with remaining marinade ingredients. Rub all over fish, stuffing the rest inside. Place inside slow cooker and cook on high 40 to 60 minutes, until cooked through at thickest point. Don't overcook or flesh will get mushy.

Serve with liquid from crock. Garnish with cilantro.

{ WITH EXTRA EFFORT } Heat 2 tablespoons of peanut oil until smoky and pour over fish to crisp the skin before garnishing.

{ Desserts & Snacks }

Desserts made in a slow cooker deliver a fabulous element of surprise, as in "Look! I made this in my Crock-Pot," to which the likely response will be, "Really? Let me see that!" Slow cookers are great with recipes that normally call for a water bath, such as bread puddings and cheesecakes. They essentially act as an oven, producing quite impressive results while you're, say, taking a nap. And why not? Life is frantic enough. Let your slow cooker sweeten it a bit.

Mango Crisp
with Mac-Nut Topping
SERVES 10

T he slow cooker is a perfect tool for making fruit fillings for pies, layer cakes, parfaits, or just to serve over ice cream. In this case, mangoes make up a filling, thickened by Minute tapioca as it cooks down. The crisp topping is baked in the oven. Bake the topping in advance, time the cooking of the filling right and you can serve up a perfectly warmed dessert just as your guests are finishing dinner.

This recipe is perfect for a smaller 2-quart cooker as the fruit will cook way down in volume. If you use a larger oval cooker the filling will end up in a shallow layer, as it would in a baking pan.

7 cups diced ripe mango (about 4 pounds whole fruit)
⅔ cup unpacked brown sugar (more or less depending on sweetness of mango)
2 teaspoons lemon juice
1½ tablespoons Minute tapioca

Topping:

½ cup flour
2 tablespoons white sugar
¼ cup packed brown sugar
¼ cup butter
1 teaspoon vanilla
½ teaspoon cinnamon
¼ cup chopped macadamia nuts (may substitute almonds or pecans)

Combine mango, brown sugar, lemon juice, and tapioca in slow cooker. Cook on low 4 hours, or until fruit is very soft. If using a 2-quart cooker, stir once halfway through.

Meanwhile, make topping: Preheat oven to 350°F. Cut flour and sugars into butter. Add vanilla and cinnamon, mix in well. Stir in nuts. Spread evenly over a baking sheet in uniform clumps. Bake 15 to 20 minutes, stirring occasionally, until toasted and brown. (Topping can be baked a day or two ahead and stored in an airtight container.)

Remove mango filling to a serving dish and sprinkle with topping. If using an oval slow cooker, filling can be topped and served right out of the crock.

Chocolate Ensemada Bread Pudding Cake

SERVES 8

An ensemada is a pastry with Spanish origins, best known in Hawai'i in its Filipino version—an oversized, soft bun slathered in butter and sugar. It has no nutritional value—in fact it has negative value. So how about we make it even worse by adding chocolate! and eggs! and more sugar!

Most slow cooker recipes for bread pudding call for setting up a water bath, as you would when baking in the oven, which makes a very soft cake. This version instead emerges firm and cakelike. The ensemada brings its own butter and sugar, giving the dish a good head start.

4 to 5 ensemada buns broken in pieces to make 4½ cups
¼ cup bittersweet chocolate chips
½ cup chopped nuts, optional

Sauce:

1½ cups coconut milk
½ cup bittersweet chocolate chips
½ cup sugar
2 teaspoons cinnamon
1 teaspoon vanilla
2 eggs

Spread ensemada pieces out in baking pan and let dry overnight, turning once.

Grease a 2-quart slow cooker (see note). Line with large square of foil, letting foil extend above the rim to help remove cooked cake.

Place ensemada pieces in mixing bowl and toss with ¼ cup chocolate chips and nuts, if using.

To make sauce: Heat coconut milk over medium heat (do not let boil). Add chocolate chips and sugar, stir to dissolve. Stir in cinnamon and vanilla.

Whisk eggs in separate bowl. Add a spoonful of the milk mixture, whisking to warm eggs. Slowly add remaining milk, whisking to combine so eggs do not curdle. Pour mixture over bread pieces and toss to coat. Spoon into crock. Cook on low 3 hours, until firm. A knife inserted into pudding should come out clean except for a possible smear of chocolate. Turn off heat, remove lid and let cool 30 minutes.

Use foil to lift bread pudding onto serving plate. It will be firm enough to slice in wedges like a cake.

{ NOTE } If you don't have a mini-cooker, this pudding can be cooked in a 2-quart baking dish that fits inside a 6- or 7-quart slow cooker. Or, double the recipe and cook it in a larger crock. Cooking time may be an hour longer.

Liliko'i Cheesecake

C heesecakes "bake" up beautifully in a slow cooker, although you can't make the standard 10-inch size. You will need a round baking dish that fits in your slow cooker. A 1½ or 2-quart casserole fits nicely in larger cookers, either oval or round, and produces a cute 8-inch cheesecake perfect for smaller parties. You'll be pouring boiling water into the cooker and lowering the casserole into the water, creating a water bath that will give your cheesecake its silky texture.

16 ounces cream cheese, softened
¾ cup sugar
1 tablespoon flour
½ cup half-and-half
2 large eggs
¼ cup liliko'i (passion fruit) purée
1 teaspoon vanilla

Crust:

¾ cup graham cracker crumbs
1 tablespoon melted butter

Line a 2-quart baking dish with large square of foil, extending above rim; grease foil. Bring 2 cups water to boil.

Combine cracker crumbs with butter; press into bottom of baking dish.

Whip cream cheese until smooth. Beat in sugar and flour, then half-and-half and eggs until mixture is smooth. Stir in liliko'i and vanilla. Pour into baking dish.

Pour boiling water into a 6- or 7-quart slow cooker. Slowly ease baking dish into cooker. Drape a clean towel over cooker so that condensation will not drip onto cheesecake. Place lid over towel. Cook on high 2 to 3 hours, until cheesecake is set. Turn off cooker and remove lid and towel. Let cheesecake sit in cooker as it cools to allow it to firm up. Top will collapse slightly. Chill well.

Unmold by grasping the edges of the foil and lifting the whole cake out of the baking dish and onto a serving dish.

{ VARIATIONS } Any type of fruit purée can be substituted for the liliko'i, or eliminate the purée and make a vanilla cheese-cake (you may need to add a little more half-and-half to the batter to make it smooth enough).

Coconut Pudding with Tapioca Pearls

MAKES 8 DESSERT CUPS

T apioca pearls are tiny globules made from tapioca starch that balloon up once cooked to resemble fish eggs. A pudding made with pearls thickens without the use of flour or cornstarch, the pearls being a starch in themselves. It's easy—and a slow cooker makes it even easier by eliminating any danger of scorching. This dish is portioned for a small, 2-quart slow cooker.

½ cup small pearl tapioca (sold in Asian markets)
3 cups water
Pinch salt
1 (13-ounce) can coconut milk
½ cup sugar
1 teaspoon vanilla extract
¼ cup guava or passion fruit juice
1 cup chopped fruit (mango, banana, strawberries, honeydew
   melon, kiwi or lychee are all good)

Place tapioca pearls and water in 2-quart slow cooker. Add salt. Cook on high until pearls turn from white to translucent, 2 to 3 hours. Don't be concerned if nothing seems to be happening for the first hour. The heat has to rise enough for the water to simmer.

Mixture will be thick and sticky; stir well, then add coconut milk and sugar. (If coconut milk has been chilled, warm in microwave before adding.) Stir until sugar dissolves. Add vanilla. Taste, adding more sugar if necessary. Divide among 8 dessert cups. Chill until firm.

Pour a thin layer of juice over each cup of pudding. Top with fruit.

{ VARIATION } Stir ¼ cup fruit purée into pudding with vanilla. Strawberries, peaches, guava, or passion fruit are good options.

{ NOTE } This recipe yields a pudding that is quite firm once chilled, relaxing a little as it sits at room temperature. For a softer pudding, soak pearls in water 10 minutes, drain, then put pearls in slow cooker with fresh water. This will remove some of the starch.

Mac-Nut Gingerbread Loaf

MAKES 1 LOAF

Not to state the obvious, but the holidays are a busy time. Let your slow cooker help you through, by assigning it a task that it can accomplish on its own while you run around for a couple of hours taking care of business.

With this cake you'll come home to the scent of gingerbread, which will make the holidays that much brighter.

This recipe is based on an idea in *Slow Cooker Desserts* by Roxanne Wyss and Kathy Moore (St. Martin's Griffin, $21.99).

1½ cups flour
¼ cup packed brown sugar
3 tablespoons white sugar
1½ teaspoons ground ginger
½ teaspoon ground cinnamon
¼ teaspoon ground cloves
¾ teaspoon baking soda
¼ teaspoon baking powder
Dash salt
6 tablespoons unsalted butter, melted
½ cup buttermilk (or ½ cup milk and ½ tablespoon vinegar)
½ cup molasses
1 large egg, at room temperature
½ cup chopped macadamia nuts

Butter and flour an 8 × 4-inch loaf pan. Place a rack in bottom of a large slow cooker (at least 5 quarts).

Whisk together flour, sugars, spices, baking soda, baking powder and salt.

In separate bowl, whisk together butter, buttermilk, molasses and egg. Pour into flour mixture and stir until blended. Stir in nuts.

Pour batter into prepared pan. Place on top of rack in slow cooker.

Cook on high 2½ to 3 hours, until a pick inserted in center comes out clean.

Cool on rack 10 minutes. Serve warm or at room temperature.

{ NOTE } Use baking parchment to make it easier to unmold the cake: Cut a strip wide enough to cover the bottom of the pan and long enough to lay across it and extend over the sides. You'll be able to use the parchment as a sling to lift out the cake. This cake can also be made in a round 2-quart casserole dish set inside a 6- to 7-quart slow-cooker.

Chocolate Mochi Cake

SERVES 12

C hewier than a cake but not as fudgy as a brownie, a slice of mochi cake is "bouncy," says Beth An Nishijima of Nori's Saimin & Snacks in Hilo, who developed this beloved snack. The Nori's version is baked in loaf pans. This is basically a half-recipe with a couple of adjustments for the slow cooker.

2¼ cups mochiko
2¼ cups sugar
2½ tablespoons unsweetened
   cocoa powder
1 teaspoon baking powder
1 (13-ounce) can coconut milk
2 eggs, beaten
½ tablespoon vanilla extract
¼ cup butter, melted

Line a 1½- or 2-quart round ceramic baking dish with large square of foil, allowing foil to extend above the rim of the dish (cake will rise all the way to the rim).

Combine mochiko, sugar, cocoa powder, and baking powder. Whisk to combine evenly. In a separate bowl combine coconut milk, eggs, vanilla extract, and butter. Add to dry mixture and stir until batter is smooth. Pour batter into baking dish and place dish in a 6- or 7-quart slow cooker. Cook on high 3 hours, until set in center. Remove lid and let cake set as the cooker cools.

Remove dish from cooker. When cake is cooled, remove from dish by lifting the foil. Peel off foil and cut cake into pieces with plastic knife.

Easy Zenzai

SERVES 12

*Z*enzai, a sweet soup of azuki beans, is a simple treat made with dried beans, water, and sugar. The end result is greater than the sum of its parts, though— ask anyone with an affinity for this Japanese dessert.

Star-Advertiser *reader Jane Wakukawa offered this slow-cooker version that calls for cooking the beans overnight, then adding sugar. Mochi balls are made on the stovetop, then stirred in. (If you want to simplify, buy mochi, cut it into squares and add it to the beans.)*

2 cups (1 16-ounce package) dry azuki beans, available in the Asian aisle of most supermarkets
8 cups water
1 cup sugar
1½ teaspoons salt

Mochi balls:

1 cup mochiko (rice flour)
4 teaspoons sugar
Pinch salt
½ cup cold water, as needed

Rinse beans, then place in 4- to 6-quart slow cooker. Add water. Cook on low 8 hours or overnight, until tender.

Spoon out excess liquid, based on how soupy you like your beans. Add sugar and salt; cook on low 30 minutes. Taste, add more sugar if desired, cook another 30 minutes.

To make mochi balls: Bring a small pot of water to boil. Combine mochiko, sugar, and salt. Add cold water a little at a time, just to moisten dough. Form into little balls and drop into boiling water; they will rise to the surface when cooked. Add mochi balls to azuki mixture.

{ NOTE } A half recipe cooks up very nicely in a 1.5- to 2-quart slow cooker.

Author Bios

Betty Shimabukuro is a managing editor at the *Honolulu Star-Advertiser* and writer of the weekly column "By Request." Her experience in food writing began in 1998 after a long career in newswriting and editing, although her cooking experience began in the kitchen with her mother, Betty Zane Shimabukuro, a legendary home economist with the University of Hawai'i's Cooperative Extension Service.

Betty is a graduate of the UH journalism program and Kaiser High School. She has worked in daily newspapers since 1979, beginning with the *Pacific Daily News* on Guam, followed by jobs in Florida and California. She met her husband, Rob, on Guam and they have three children, Justin, Christine, and Caleb, plus a gigantic dog named Jax who is happy to clean up all failed cooking experiments.

Previous cookbooks:

As author: *By Request, By Request 2,* and *By Request Highlights*

As co-author (with Muriel Miura): *What Hawai'i Likes to Eat, Hawai'i's Holiday Cookbook,* and *Favorite Recipes From What Hawai'i Likes to Eat.*

Honolulu Star-Advertiser food editor Joleen Oshiro was born in Honolulu and raised in Waipahu. A graduate of Waipahu High School and the University of Hawai'i, Joleen had her first encounter with journalism during a career day event at Waipahu High when she invited then-*Honolulu Star-Bulletin* executive editor John Simonds to speak about the profession. During her freshman year at UH in 1983, Simonds offered her a job at the *Star-Bulletin* and she became the paper's copygirl. She has worked in Hawai'i newspapers ever since, as a page designer, copy editor, and arts writer before stepping into the world of food. Joleen lives in Waikele with her husband, Noel, and daughter, Mia.

Previous cookbook:

As co-editor (with Betty Shimabukuro): *Hawai'i's Ohana Cookbook*

Pressure Cooking References

I have found several resources invaluable in navigating the pressure cooker, and I recommend them to anyone who wants to delve into the world of pressure cooking.

Books

- *Pressure Perfect: Two Hour Taste in Twenty Minutes Using Your Pressure Cooker,* by Lorna Sass (2004, William Morrow Cookbooks, $24.99)
- *Cooking Under Pressure, 20th Anniversary Edition*, by Sass (2009, William Morrow Cookbooks, $23.99)
- Sass has also published various vegetarian and vegan pressure-cooker cookbooks, as well as one focusing on whole grains.

Cooking Class

- Chef Alyssa Moreau teaches non-credit culinary classes at Kapiʻolani Community College (continuinged.kcc.hawaii.edu). She also teaches private group and individualized classes. Contact Moreau at www.divinecreationshawaii.com

Online

- "Pressure Cooking with Lorna Sass" (pressurecookingwithlornasass.wordpress.com)
- "Miss Vickie's Pressure Cooking Recipes" (missvickie.com)

Slow Cooking Resources

This book focuses on local-style recipes, but the slow cooker offers a world of possibilities beyond that. To build on your repertoire, I suggest these sources, from opposite ends of the culinary spectrum. They were major inspirations on my Crock-Pot crusade:

- Stephanie O'Dea is a home cook who created the blog "A Year of Slow Cooking" (crockpot365.blogspot.com), based on her mission to use her Crock-Pot every day of 2008. She also has two *Make It Fast Cook It Slow* cookbooks published by Hyperion. Both books and blog, and the first recipes I made following her examples, persuaded me that my slow cooker relationship was worth pursuing. O'Dea continues to update her blog with new recipes. For beginners to this type of cooking, her work is a great launching point.

- *Slow Cooker Revolution* was written and published by the editors of America's Test Kitchen, whom I have always imagined to be an odd bunch of obsessive perfectionists. They purchased more than two-dozen slow cookers so that they could test continuously, redoing recipes at high heat, low heat, with browning, without browning and with any number of ingredient options. I learned a lot from their suggestions on cooking technique and bumping up flavor. Since *Slow Cooker Revolution* was published in 2011, the editors have come out with a second volume of *Revolution*, as well as *Healthy Slow Cooker Revolution* and *The Complete Slow Cooker*. I strongly suggest these books for those who want to go beyond the basics and learn to really coax the best out of their devices.

Pressure Cooker Index

BY TIME

Slow Cooker Index
BY TIME

Index

Notes

Other Best-Selling

Star ★ Advertiser
Cookbooks

176 pp. • 6 × 9 in. • softcover

208 pp. • 6 × 9 in. • hardcover

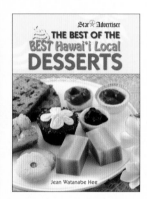

192 pp. • 6 × 9 in. • softcover

180 pp. • 6 × 9 in. • hardcover